THE
CHOICE

The
Choice

Eliyahu M. Goldratt

Additional copies can be obtained from your local book-
store or the publisher:

The North River Press
Publishing Corporation
P.O. Box 567
Great Barrington, MA 01230
(800) 486.2665 or (413) 528.0034

www.northriverpress.com

ISBN: 978-0-88427-189-5

Printed in the United States of America

Dedication

To Efrat,

Some might say:
-That it's not easy to work with a perfectionist.
-That it's quite irritating to rewrite almost every page.
-That it's frustrating to debate for hours on a single word.
-That it's nerve-wracking when 'good enough' is not an option.

Not me.

Why bother if the writing does not accurately reflect my approach?
Why bother if the words I put in your mouth are not okay with you?
Why bother if the end result is open to misinterpretations?
Why bother if the book is not easily readable?

But, above all, I enjoyed the "duels."

Thank you!

P. S. Shall we do it again?

Contents

Foreword

Eli Goldratt is probably best known by his millions of readers as a business guru. Those who know him a little better may think of him as a scientist and an educator, and to some he is a genius, a classification he vehemently denies. To me he is all that and, of course, much more. I have been Eli's publisher, editor and friend for over twenty-five years.

Early on I was aware that Eli is actually on a quest to demonstrate that the approach and methods of the hard sciences can and should be applied to the social sciences. He initially targeted management science, claiming that since in that branch of the social sciences results are measurable, people find it harder to dispute the superiority of using the hard science techniques. It was fascinating to see how gradually the business world accepted Eli's work in spite of the fact that so much of it is a drastic departure from tradition. His Theory of Constraints (TOC) is now taught at almost every business school and MBA program and has been used by thousands of companies and government agencies worldwide. TOC has been successfully applied in almost every area of human endeavor, from industry to health care to education.

Unlike his readers, I have had the opportunity to see Eli in action. Together we struggled in an industry—the publishing industry—that views itself as so unique that its self-imposed limitations are almost written in stone. As of this writing we have published nine books together; books that have been translated into twenty-seven languages, and sold many millions of copies. We have had tremendous success, outselling many bestsellers by far and keeping an undiminished market for our books. Eli's first book, *The Goal*, sells as many copies per year now as it did twenty years ago. Taking into account the millions of used copies available, this is a remarkable feat. Of course we made mistakes along the way, but each mistake led to new thought, new approaches, new ways, which in turn led to more success.

What I realized through that struggle is that Eli has developed much more than he was writing about. I became convinced that he developed a pragmatic life philosophy that guides not just his writing but also all his conduct. It's no wonder that I started to press him to share, in writing, his unique approach. For years, actually decades, he declined, claiming that he was not yet ready. At last I prevailed. This book is the result. I hope you enjoy and benefit from it as much as I do.

Laurence Gadd
The North River Press

THE
CHOICE

CHAPTER 1

What Choice Do We Have?

My name is Efrat. I'm accustomed to reading my father's writing out loud to him. He claims that my comments, and more so my body language, help him to spot when his arguments are unclear.

Once I asked him, "Why me?"

"Because, unlike so many other people, you don't fool yourself that you know everything about organizations, let alone about human behavior."

I like his answer. I worked hard to get a Ph.D. in organizational psychology. I invested many years to learn how much we don't know. No wonder the title of this report, which I am about to read aloud to him, is of particular interest to me. It's called "Freedom of Choice."

"Father, what is the choice you made that impacted your life the most?" I ask.

Decisively he answers, "I wanted to live a full life. The most important decision that led directly to it was my decision to constantly devote time to understanding, really understanding, each one of my areas of interest: family, friends and work."

Knowing that when Father says "really understand,"

he means spending endless hours in the attempt to decipher the causalities that govern a situation, I sigh, "That's not easy."

"Who is talking about easy? Do you want an easy life?" he asks.

Being the daughter of my father I have heard this question more than once. "I know, I know. If you want an easy life just grab a hammer, a big one, and hit yourself on the head, hard. You'll have a very easy life. They'll even bring the food to your bed."

I definitely want to live a meaningful life—a full life—and so does everyone I know.

I'm also aware that even though people want to live a full life, most people don't achieve it.

"Why is it so difficult for people to admit that they don't want an easy life?" he asks.

"Because, they do want an easier life, and living a meaningful life is so difficult to reach."

He gestures impatiently with his hand. "There are ways to make it more attainable. It only requires one to think. To think clearly. To think like a true scientist."

"In other words," I say cynically, "you just have to be born a genius."

He immediately responds, "No, you don't. I was not born with any exceptional brainpower and I have my IQ results from my youth to confirm it. I am a bodybuilder. Practice, practice, practice. Efrat, when will you realize that you, like every other person, have enough intuition and brainpower to think like a true scientist?"

I don't buy it. But there is something else in Father's decisiveness that bothers me even more. "Father, in what way does thinking like a true scientist enable a person to live a full life?"

He grins, and true to his Socratic approach, rather than answering he asks, "Maybe you can deduce the answer from the report we intended to start reading fifteen minutes ago?"

I start to read.

The report is about what has been taking up almost all his time over the past few weeks. It all started with a coincidence—two retail chains expressed interest in implementing his theory. Within two weeks it had grown into a major opportunity involving five of the largest retail chains in Brazil. Then, exactly when he was starting to steer his group into this new and incredibly promising segment, it crumbled into nothing.*

When I finish, he asks, "Well?"

"What a disappointment it must be for you," I say.

"Why are you talking about disappointment?" he asks in a surprised voice.

I firmly say, "Everybody feels a sense of disappointment when an initiative doesn't work. The more important the initiative, the bigger the disappointment. Even when a person makes the right choice, even when a person is optimistic and chooses to look on the bright side, even when the person is made out of iron, he or she will be disappointed. The fact that you repress these feelings doesn't mean that they don't exist."

He smiles. "A typical argument from a psychologist. Now that you claim that I just repress my feelings of disappointment, how can I be taken seriously when I say that I don't feel any?"

I dismiss his remark; I know that I'm right.

"Let's view it from a different angle," he suggests. "Let's suppose that you are a scientist and you are trying to build an instrument that is based on a new approach. Of course, being experienced, you will first do an exper-

---

*For the curious reader, the report in full is in the appendix.

iment; you will build a prototype. What would you expect from the prototype?"

I choose my words carefully. "Only a fool expects a prototype to work perfectly the first time. What one expects is to find out what does work according to expectations, and what doesn't."

"Well put," he encourages me. "Now, suppose that the prototype verifies a few new things that do work, and reveals one thing that doesn't work. Since one thing was not working, the prototype, as an instrument, did not work well or didn't work at all. Do you suppose, my dear daughter, that you, the scientist who built the prototype, would feel disappointed?"

I see where he is leading. It's interesting. "Just a little bit," I say.

"And once you figure out how to fix the things that were not working? How would you feel then?"

"I would feel energized," I admit.

For my father, every situation is an opportunity to learn, every new initiative is an exploration. I glance over the document I have just read. It's evident that he was constructing and experimenting as he moved along. The analogy of a prototype is appropriate.

"What's the difference between the scientist who designs a prototype of an instrument and any other person who just uses the instruments?" he asks.

That's an easy question. Confidently I answer, "Most people don't know much about the inner workings of an instrument; for them the instrument is just a box. So if it doesn't work, they will feel disappointment. If they need it to work, then they won't just be disappointed, they will be frustrated."

He nods in agreement.

"As for the scientist," I continue, "he knows how and why the instrument works; he is familiar with the components of the instrument; he understands the cause-and-effect relationships that make it work. Therefore, even if the prototype, as an instrument, didn't work, as long as it provided new knowledge of which cause-and-effects are valid and which are not, the satisfaction of making progress compensates for the disappointment."

Father leans forward and says, "When a prototype—a new initiative—doesn't work, we face two alternatives: one is to bitch about reality and the other is to harvest the gift it just gave us, the knowledge of what has to be corrected. That is the reason I titled the report Freedom of Choice."

Before I have time to digest, he continues, "But enough talking about instruments and prototypes. Let's talk about reality; the reality you just read about. Do you still think that I was disappointed?"

After a short silence he repeats his question. "Efrat, do you still think that I was disappointed?"

Finally I answer, "You were probably fine, but I'm sure that the people around you were deeply disappointed."

"You're right," he admits.

"And I bet it wasn't easy for you to help them overcome their disappointment. I have no doubt that it drained their energy and that you had to work hard to revive their enthusiasm and determination. 'Freedom of choice' you call it. Well, for you it might be easy, but for most people it is quite difficult to make the productive choice."

After a while he asks, "Why?"

"Why is it difficult for everybody or why is it easy for you?"

"Why is it different for me?"

Hesitantly I answer, "You're always the scientist. You are constantly figuring out how the world is ticking, trying to verbalize the cause-and-effect connections—on any subject, in any situation." I continue more confidently, "For you, everything is like a prototype. No wonder situations that trigger disappointment and frustration for others are, for you, a source of energy."

This is a new realization for me. It is evident that the approach of a scientist gives a substantial advantage. But what is that approach?

On the one hand, one has to be humble to assume that one doesn't know. Actually, to avoid feeling disappointed, one has to expect that things will, most probably, not work the first time.

On the other hand, one must be arrogant; have the confidence that one is capable of figuring out how to make things work.

Put these two requirements together and you have a nice oxymoron: humble arrogance.

Looking at Father I say, "This is the first time that I've become aware of how helpful the scientist's approach can be in maintaining the stamina needed to go after new initiatives."

"It is also helpful in generating the initiatives to start with," he comments.

"Probably," I say.

Father doesn't like such a noncommittal response.

"Do you agree with what Seneca said two thousand years ago, that 'good luck is preparation meets opportunity'?" he asks.

I slowly say, "And knowing the causes and effects that govern a situation is the best preparation."

Father continues to guide me. "What happens if someone is not prepared; if he is blind to the stream of opportunities that reality is presenting to him?"

It's not too difficult to predict the outcome. "If someone isn't prepared, then he won't see most of the opportunities. Such a person will be waiting for good luck to provide everything on a silver platter." Taking it further I continue, "And if a person doesn't have enough opportunities he will feel that life didn't give him a fair chance, that he is constrained by circumstances, that he is powerless."

How many of my friends have I just described?

Isn't it too simplistic? I have to think more about it.

"Bad luck is reality meets lack of preparation," he concludes. "Approaching reality like a scientist, if done well, also provides the needed preparation."

Then he adds, "If someone is not prepared, what freedom of choice does he have?"

I now start to realize that it isn't just the freedom to choose the bright side. Freedom of choice is also connected to the ability to recognize situations that can be turned into real opportunities.

Father interrupts my thoughts with a big sigh, "Unfortunately, in spite of all my efforts, too often I find myself unprepared."

I smile. I wish I could be as unprepared as he is. To make sure I understand I try to put things in order.

"The fact that you are constantly building logical maps of reality helps you in two ways. First of all, and now I am starting to realize how crucial this is, you are able to recognize opportunities in the areas that are important to you. And secondly, when they initially don't work, you don't lose energy. On the contrary, the missing element is sticking out, and you enthusiastically charge to complete it and turn the opportunity into a success. I've seen you do it again and again."

After a short while I add, "I envy you. I wish that I had inherited your genius."

"Here we go again," he sighs. "Every person is born with tremendous brainpower. Unfortunately, there are obstacles that stand in the way of using that brainpower.

The deeper meaning of freedom of choice is the choice to invest in overcoming these obstacles."

Seeing that I don't have a problem with this he continues. "Can you speculate what these obstacles are?"

As a psychologist my list of potential obstacles is endless; there are numerous psychological barriers. Rather than listing them, I ask, "Can you give me a clue?"

"The more complicated the situation seems to be, the simpler the solution must be," he recites. It's one of his favorite phrases.

Now I'm stuck. I'm used to approaching it from the inner working of a person, from his emotions, from his inhibitions. Father wants me to approach it from the outside; from the reality that the person struggles with.

Rather than giving an off-the-cuff answer, I ask, "What are the obstacles?"

He takes his time lighting his pipe. When he is pleased with the resulting gray cloud he starts. "The first and most profound obstacle is that people believe that reality is complex, and therefore they are looking for sophisticated explanations for complicated solutions. Do you understand how devastating this is?"

"I have a hunch but I'd rather have you explain."

"I'm looking for a good analogy," he says while his eyes search the ceiling. "Suppose that you have an excellent screwdriver, and you need to take out a screw from a piece of wood. You have the right tool for the task, but for some reason, you think that it's not a screw but a nail. How successful will you be? In such a case, to claim that you don't have a good enough tool is ridiculous. There is nothing wrong with people's brainpower; there is something very wrong with people's perception of reality. The biggest obstacle is that people grasp reality as complex when actually it is surprisingly simple."

When he sees that I get it, he continues, "When I

left physics and started to deal with organizations I was astonished to see that the attitude of most people is that the more sophisticated something is, the more respectable it is. This ridiculous fascination with sophistication also causes people to altogether avoid using their brainpower. You see, since complicated solutions never work, people tell themselves that they don't know enough, that a lot of detailed knowledge is needed before one can even attempt to understand an environment."

"I know a few such sad cases," I concur.

"The admiration of sophistication is totally wrong," he firmly continues. "The key for thinking like a true scientist is the acceptance that any real life situation, no matter how complex it initially looks, is actually, once understood, embarrassingly simple. Moreover, if the situation is based on human interactions, you probably already have enough knowledge to begin with."

"I'm not sure that I agree with your latter statement," I say. "And I think that most people, taking their personal life as a reference, will not agree even with your former one."

"How can I convince you?" he asks.

Since I have never fully accepted Father's claim that complex reality is actually simple, I decide to use this opportunity to get to the bottom of it, once and for all. "Give me an example, a decisive one," I insist.

"Fine," he says. "Pick something that you struggle with."

No, this is too easy. I, too, am able to find elegant solutions to personal problems. Sometimes. "Picking something that I struggle with will not be a meaningful example for anybody but me," I object. And then I clarify. "It will not be enough for anybody else because everyone thinks that their personal problems are not only unique, but that they are the most difficult to overcome, if they can be overcome at all. Therefore, picking something that I struggle with will not convince anybody else that the same can be done for the situations they are facing."

"Let's start with convincing you," he smiles. "That's hard enough."

"But that won't be a good example even for me," I continue to object. "I don't buy that for any situation that is based on human interactions I already have enough knowledge to begin with. Picking something that I struggle with will not cause me to change my mind, because in that situation, it is likely that I already have plenty of knowledge to begin with."

"What example will satisfy you?" he moans. "You do not accept any personal problem but you still want the example to be on peoples' problematic situations. Maybe we can agree on the following approach. You must agree that no man is an island; most of a person's difficulties and joys stem from his interactions with other human beings."

I don't have a problem with that. He continues, "The more complicated cases are cases that involve not just one person, but many people, each with his unique personality, self-interests and preconceived notions. The most difficult cases are those dealing not just with a diverse group, but also with a diverse group that has to achieve something together. In other words, an organization."

I don't agree that an organization is more complicated than a single person, but I like the idea that rather than using an example of a specific personal problem, Father will try to demonstrate his claims using organizations.

I take over. "So what you suggest is that you'll take a specific organization and show me that it is actually simple to understand how and why it behaves the way it does. But you also claim that clear thinking helps to generate opportunities. So it will not be enough that you just take a specific organization and decipher the cause-and-effect relationships that govern its activities. You also have to show me that through the simple logical map you have built, new opportunities are opened. The bigger the better."

Before he can comment I remind him of the real challenge. "You also claimed that if the situation is based on human interactions, I already have enough knowledge to decipher how and why it works; its governing causalities. Every organization is based on human interaction, so for me to check if your claim is correct, choose a type of organization that I've never worked with."

He doesn't seem to be disturbed. "Have you ever worked with really complex organizations, the billions-of-dollars companies?"

"I can't even comprehend the meaning of a billion dollars," I admit.

"What about the apparel industry?" he inquires. "Have you ever looked into the inner workings of one of the big brand names?"

"No, I haven't."

He turns to his laptop and after a while he says, "I just transferred a file to you. It's a report about a very large and successful apparel company. But we have to agree about what will convince you that it is a good example, namely that the governing cause-and-effect relationships are simple. Embarrassingly simple."

"That's easy; if they are not embarrassingly simple I'll get lost," I smile, "and bored."

"Fair enough," he laughs. "I'm confident to the extent that I'm willing to bet that not only will you not be bored, you'll be flabbergasted that the managers of that company, and the managers of almost any other similar company, have not seen the obvious before."

"What are we betting?" I jokingly ask.

"Something big," he answers. "The prize that you'll win is a firsthand realization of the extent to which the governing causalities are nothing but common sense. And how powerful this common sense is."

"Knowing you, it will probably be uncommon sense," I say, smiling as I open the file.

CHAPTER 2

Uncommon Sense*

A few weeks ago, I spent a morning with a group of more than twenty middle-level managers from a major brand in apparel. We will call the company BigBrand. My reason for writing this report is the annoying feeling that you think that there is a limit to how much a company can improve; that a quantum jump in performance is possible for only small and maybe medium-sized companies. But when it comes to very large companies (the billions-of-dollars companies), an improvement of the magnitude of, for example, bringing their yearly net profit to be equal to their current annual sales in just a few years, is really beyond a realistic possibility.

BigBrand is one of the best companies in existence. There

---

* A report to the Goldratt Group, April 2006. For the purpose of this book this report was slightly modified to enable easy comprehension for readers who are not familiar with the Theory of Constraints.

are very few people who haven't heard about BigBrand, and when you examine their financial performance you see that their reputation is well-founded. Their annual sales are several billion U.S. dollars and their net profit on sales is about ten percent. To make about ten percent net profit on sales in the apparel industry is very good.

My first question to the group was, "By how much do you think you can increase your net profit? What will your net profit be, let's say, five years from now?"

There was a lot of debate in the room until the top gun—the director of finance—spoke up. His decisive answer was that in five years they would almost double their net profit to one billion dollars per year. They are aware that it is quite an ambitious target, and they know it is not going to be easy. Nevertheless, as a company they are determined that yes, they can make it. That ended the debate.

Rather than starting to explore how they are going to achieve this ambitious target, I preferred to ask if they think that in five years they can reach a four-billion-dollar net profit per year. Not surprisingly, they didn't need any guidance answering this question. They made it clear this number is totally, utterly unrealistic.

Is it unrealistic?

Increasing net profit can be achieved either through expansion or through improvement of the existing operation. I agree that for a large company to expand fivefold in a few years is unrealistic. What about increasing net profit through improving the existing operations?

Like almost any other company, they, too have numerous initiatives for improvement. And like almost any other company, most improvement initiatives are centered mainly on cost savings—including trying to save on transportation and trying to find cheaper, yet still acceptable, suppliers. If a cost-saving program generates savings of a few million a year it is regarded as a good initiative. If it saves tens of millions a year it is regarded as exceptionally successful. It's no wonder that they regard increasing net profit by billions as impossible.

To reveal the true potential for improvement I wanted them to examine the phenomenon of shortages; of missing items.

"A shop has a list of the items or SKUs (stock keeping units) it has decided to hold. On average, what percentage of these SKUs is missing from the shops?" I asked.

Like in many other brand environments, where management knows that shortages (out-of-stock situations) are prevalent but doesn't have a clear idea of the magnitude, their speculation was that it is probably close to thirty percent.

"How much do you lose in sales at the shops due to unavailability of products?" I asked.

"Less than thirty percent," was their answer. "Because, many times, a customer who cannot find one product will still buy an alternative product."

I voiced my disagreement. I acknowledged that some customers do buy an alternative product, but there is another factor that caused me to believe that the lost sales are much higher than the percentage of SKUs that are missing.

"Is there anything that typifies the articles that are missing from the shops?" I asked.

They didn't have any trouble in answering that the missing articles are the ones for which demand was much higher than forecasted.

"Can we conclude that the demand for the missing items is above the average level of demand for most items available?" I asked.

Considering the fact that so many of the items available in the shop are slow movers, they had to agree.

The next rhetorical question was, "Doesn't it mean that the effect on lost sales is much higher than the percentage of missing items?"

When many had speculated that lost sales might be as high as fifty percent, I added, "If we take as a base the existing sales, doesn't it mean that the amount you lose due to shortages is close to what you are actually selling?"

That shook them a bit. I continued to unfold the picture by drawing their attention to their warehouses. Items missing from BigBrand's warehouses are erased from the list of items that the shop should hold. Therefore, it is important to also investigate the additional impact of shortages at the warehouses.

Products of BigBrand, like so many fashion products,

have a lifetime in the market of six months; their business is based on two seasons a year. Therefore, every six months they launch a new collection. They order and buy in batches of six months—for the whole season. My question to them was, "If one enters your central warehouse in a given region, three weeks after the beginning of the season, will he find that some SKUs are already missing from the warehouse?"

Their answer was, "Yes, definitely."

"How can it be that these articles are already missing from the central warehouse after three weeks, when at the beginning of the season there was a quantity stored that was anticipated to last six months?"

Again, the answer was that these missing articles are the real high runners, the hot ones, the ones for which demand was much higher than forecasted.

"How much in sales is lost from these items not being available?"

We went over the following chain of logic. If an item was depleted in one month, they actually lost its sales during the next five months. The lost sales of that item are probably equal to five times the amount that was sold (they agreed that, usually, demand for an item at the beginning of the season is not a peak but a reflection of genuine market demand).

"How many items are depleted after three weeks? After six weeks? After three months?"

They didn't have numerical answers, but their impression was that the number of items depleted within the first three months of the season is very significant. They would not be surprised if it is typically equal to one-third of all SKUs.

As we said, items missing from a brand's warehouses are erased from the list of items that the shops should hold. Therefore, we should combine the impact of missing items in the shops with the impact of missing items in the warehouses. They agreed that we are dealing here with a phenomenon that is, most probably, equal to or higher than the total amount of realized sales.

Then I encouraged them to convert this realization into the bottom line impact; to estimate how big of an impact shortages have on the net profit of the company. I asked, "If the company succeeds in eliminating shortages, by how much should it expect its net profit to increase?"

After some discussion, they reached the conclusion that if by some miracle the shops will not suffer from any shortages, BigBrand would need to increase only modestly its infrastructure to support the resulting increase in sales; that the resulting increase in sales would not be associated with a meaningful increase in operating expenses. The only cost that would go up is the amount of money they will have to pay their suppliers for the additional goods. But since they purchase the goods for a price that is only one-fifth of their selling price, eighty percent of the money generated by the increase in sales resulting from the reduction in shortages goes directly to the bottom line.

There was quiet in the room when the unavoidable conclusion crystallized: eliminating shortages has an impact on net profit that is probably larger than four billion dollars a year.

How come they had not fully realized it before?

I shared with them my speculation that it stems from their particular environment. The culture in that industry is dominated by the fact that for several generations they have been dealing with an environment in which the lifetime of the products in the market (six months) is shorter than the time to supply (one-and-a-half years). For example, the fabric is selected by the brand companies in January or February for the *next* year's summer season. This is an extremely difficult environment to deal with, as more and more industries (e.g. electronics) that are drifting into such an environment are starting to painfully realize.

No wonder that, with time, this industry developed a protective mechanism; a culture of camouflaging the painful problems so that they can be embraced. For example, how does the industry cope with the phenomenon of huge sales losses on items that become unavailable long before the end of the season? They do not give it a name that clearly shows the negative impact. Instead they camouflage it with a positive title. They call it "sold out." They all laughed when they admitted they actually regard "sold out" as something positive.

In the same way, the industry hides from itself the phenomenon that is the other side of the same coin. The terms obsolescence and obsolete products do not exist in this industry. Together we explored how the fashion industry hides the obsolescence from itself.

At the brand level it is hidden under the title "outlet sales." What is the reduction in price given in the outlet? It is never in the range of five to ten percent. It is a minimum of thirty percent, and a seventy percent reduction is quite common. This merchandise is merchandise that the brands are stuck with and are unable to push into retail.

On top of that, there is the obsolescence in the inventory the retailers are holding. Once again, it is not called obsolescence, it is called end-of-the-season clearance sale. Again, the price reduction offered at an end-of-the-season sale is above the range of five to ten percent. And this sale starts at least a month, if not two, before the end of the season.

The amount of obsolescence in the system is probably equal to thirty percent or more of the total items produced. This is not a small phenomenon.

What we must bear in mind is that these two phenomena coexist. For a huge number of SKUs there are considerable shortages, while at the same time, for not a smaller number of SKUs there are enormous surpluses.

"How come?"

They didn't have much trouble answering; the answer is obvious to anybody in the trade.

When do they decide on the quantities to be produced of each SKU? Before the beginning of the season. Do they know, at that stage, what the actual demand per SKU will be? Of course not.

The room was filled with their nasty remarks about the forecast. They ridiculed the notion that anybody can forecast, more than six months in advance, the demand on an SKU level. The forecast is not even considered, by them, to be an educated guess. No wonder that for about half the items the forecast is too low, leading to shortages, and for the other half the forecast is too high, leading to obsolescence.

But can they do anything about it?

Yes, they can, provided that they will abandon the illusion created by the forecast—the illusion that the future demand is known. How should they operate if their starting assumption is that they do not know the future demand per SKU?

We started to examine the possibilities by exploring when they can get reliable knowledge of which SKUs are moving well and which are not?

They claimed that after the first two weeks of the season they have that knowledge, but it's already too late.

Is it? What will happen if the reaction time of the supply chain is much faster?

"But currently it takes two months for the suppliers to produce the goods," they rightfully claimed.

"Why?" I asked. "Why is it that a pair of shoes or a garment that takes less than thirty minutes net time to produce should be subject to a production lead time of two months?"

"Because we order in very large quantities," was their embarrassed answer. "We order the quantity forecasted for the entire season."

"Will ordering much smaller quantities, more frequently, raise the price?"

"Not as long as the total amount ordered per season is roughly the same, or larger," was their answer. "But what about the time to transport the goods?" they asked. "Most of the production is done in the Far East."

"There are airplanes," was my flat answer.

It didn't take long before the basis of the new mode of operations was sketched out.

They could start the season with just one month of inventory and use the first two or three weeks to get real knowledge of what is moving and what is not. Based on actual consumption they would then replenish to the warehouses. Of course they would have to convince the suppliers to work with much smaller batches; not a big deal since producing apparel in smaller batches does not necessitate more capacity.

Of course, for the high runners that are revealed in the first two weeks, they will have to prepare the system to air freight the goods needed for the next few weeks as well as shipping another quantity by sea. Overall, it should be expected that less than twenty percent of the goods would be sent by air rather than sea. They quickly realized that even though transporting by air is much more expensive than sea, relative to the selling price (or even worse, relative to not selling) it is negligible.

The above, which they regarded as a major, system-wide change (though still logical and doable), will reduce the shortages to a mere fraction of what they are today, and almost eliminate the obsolescence.

There were pleased murmurs in the room when the conclusion was explicitly verbalized: this by itself is probably enough to reach the realistic target of four billion dollars per year net profit.

But we had just started.

"Let's see if we can agree on the next guiding concept," I said. "As long as the end consumer hasn't bought, nobody in the supply chain has sold."

I was surprised that they all supported that statement. They continued to support it even when I drew this blunt conclusion: Even though on the financial books BigBrand recognizes a sale whenever it delivers the goods to retail, they should not consider such a situation as if they have finished doing their job. They haven't finished until the end consumer has bought, not before.

What can they do after the goods have been delivered to the retailer? To reach the answer we examined the typical behavior of their clients.

To secure the price, the retailer buys from BigBrand in very large quantities. This purchase is also based on a long-term forecast. It is no wonder that about one-third of the products they buy are slow movers.

"Now," I asked them, "do you agree that in retail what is not displayed is not sold?"

That is almost the motto of the trade, so of course they agreed. Then we continued to draw the chain of cause and effect. When the retailer starts to realize that he is holding a lot of relatively slow movers, he also realizes that unless he does something these slow movers will be sold only at the end of the season for a loss. So what is the natural reaction? These slow movers are now getting a good visual display; visual display that is better than what they deserve. And they get the attention of the sales force more than they deserve, at the expense of the attention and display that the better runners should get. How much is lost in sales due to this? We agreed that nobody knows, but there is one thing everybody knows—it is significant.

"What will happen," I asked, "if BigBrand makes this offer to their retailers: they will accept back any merchandise for a full refund?"

Getting harsh responses from all sides, I took a step back.

When the room became quiet again I offered another question, this time choosing my words more carefully. "Once there are no shortages to speak of in the warehouses, will BigBrand be able to promise the shops a two-day delivery on any reasonable order?"

The warehouses of BigBrand are located within, maximum, a two-day drive from almost all shops. So it didn't take long for them to come to the conclusion that it is feasible to provide such service. And that it would have only a modest impact, if any, on the cost of transportation.

I highlighted that with such service, and basing the price on a shop's total sales of BigBrand products, rather than on the size of individual orders, the shops will no longer have the pressure to hold mountains of inventories. Now suppose that the shops take advantage of BigBrand's excellent service and order every day the items that were sold that day. Under those conditions, we agreed that a shop should hold only what is needed for proper visual display plus the quantity that the shop optimistically expects to sell in the following two days. Relative to today's situation the inventories that the shop would hold would be much smaller.

Now I could raise the question again. "What will then happen if BigBrand offers, to the retailers that order daily, that it will accept back any merchandise for a full refund?"

After some calmer discussion they reached the conclusion that the returns would not be too high and that they do have the outlets in place to get rid of them. Now they were willing to continue listening.

The approach is: let's make sure that the best display and the attention of the sales force is devoted to the best-selling products. Accepting back the slow movers for a full refund will go a long way toward enhancing the right behavior in retail. As long as we believe that display and a gentle push from the shops' sales force are important, we must conclude that sales will grow. How much? Their estimates of the resulting increase in sales were all over the map.

Rather than pushing for an agreed, speculative number, I stated that we could do much more. Now that our solution provides essential information we didn't have before—which SKU has sold in which shop every day—BigBrand should take an active role. It should suggest to the retailer that they send back the items that are not moving in their store. And those items that are moving nicely in other stores located in your region, take them instead. If this is done, the shops will hold on their shelves a much higher percentage of good movers. How much will sales go up? Nobody knows, but the consensus was that it's big. Very big.

All of the above set the stage for the climax, for the action that will have the biggest impact.

A store knows that a fresh collection attracts clients to the store. We discussed that it is the reason chains and shops are putting a lot of pressure on BigBrand to switch from two collections per year to four collections per year. They pointed out that considering the amount of effort and cost required, the mere fact that BigBrand now seriously considers this request shows that everyone recognizes that such a move would have a major impact on total sales.

But does BigBrand have to put forth the mammoth effort needed to provide four collections per year?

How many variations per season does BigBrand design, produce and store in their warehouses? Their surprising answer was: in the vicinity of eighty thousand variations per season. (Variation does *not* include size, so the number of SKUs produced and stored is by far larger.) I was expecting a large number, but not quite so large.

"Why such a huge number?" I asked, and they explained: it is due to the need to convince the clients, the retail chains, to buy from BigBrand. Different retailers have different tastes and predictions about the market, so BigBrand has to design, produce and store an enormous number of variations if they want to be a major supplier to so many different chains.

"And how many variations does a store hold, even a large store?"

"Of our products? Less than two thousand," was their answer.

These vastly different numbers provided the base to draw some conclusions. In almost any given store the variety of items the consumer sees is just a tiny fraction of what is actually available. Once BigBrand starts replenishing daily to the stores and accepting back items from the stores, it is possible to make sure that stores will have a new collection every month—with no increase in the number of items that BigBrand currently designs, produces and warehouses.

The head of finance provided a perfect ending when he summarized: "Reaching four billion dollars net profit per year is starting to look conservative."

CHAPTER 3

Why is Common Sense
Not Common Practice?

It is nine o'clock at night and the kids are, at last, fast asleep. I reread the document again, trying to envision BigBrand. A company that designs, orders, distributes, stores and sells the staggering number of eighty thousand variations per season is complex beyond my imagination.

Was Father right in his claim that I did have all the relevant facts needed for the analysis?

The first fact that he is using in his analysis is the magnitude of existing shortages. Did I know this before reading the report?

The answer must be yes, since from firsthand experience I know that many times the dress that I liked was not available in my size or in the right color. I never called it a "shortage" or "out-of-stock situation," but if I had to guess, I would say that I faced disappointment no less than one-quarter of the time.

And, of course, I am aware that in the summer the shops don't hold winter clothes and that last year's designs are like yesterday's newspaper.

Here is something I didn't know: I didn't know that

the brands pay the manufacturers only one-fifth of the price they charge the retailers for the garments. But, on second thought, I did know that brands' margins are very big because I know that there is a huge difference in price between buying a piece of cloth and buying a nice dress that carries the label of a known brand.

As for outlets and end-of-season sales, they are responsible for a lot of my wardrobe.

So I did have all the relevant facts. What about the cause-and-effect logic that ties these facts together to bring to light the astonishing potential for improvement? Father is right; this cause-and-effect logic is common sense. I didn't have any problem following it and I don't think that anybody else will. In hindsight it is so obvious.

I asked for a decisive example that would demonstrate that even complicated, human-based environments are governed by simple, common sense logic. And a novice knows all the needed facts. And that the understanding of that logic opens new and fruitful opportunities. I asked for a decisive example and now I must admit that I got one. So where does it leave me?

True, his cause-and-effect analysis is common sense. True, I did have all the facts. But it is also true that on my own, I would never have come up with such an analysis.

How does he come up with these elegant analyses? What gives him the ability to construct an analysis that is only obvious to others after it has been presented to them in enough detail? In short, I'm more convinced than ever that to do what he has done at BigBrand one needs exceptional brainpower.

Is exceptional brainpower really needed for reaching a full life? Most people's aspirations, mine included, are not at the level of figuring out how to propel a whole industry to a new level of performance.

But on second thought, when a person faces an undesirable situation that he or she is convinced they cannot change, they feel blocked. Succeeding in such situations requires a breakthrough, maybe not of the magnitude I just read about, but a breakthrough nevertheless. Aren't the most meaningful opportunities the ones that open when a person realizes how to overcome a constraining situation? In other words, when one reaches what is, for them, a breakthrough?

So, meaningful opportunities are open when one sees how to overcome something that blocks one; when one is able to come up with modest breakthroughs. I'm willing to contemplate that I might have enough brainpower for that and the problem is maybe I'm just not using it effectively. I'm willing to entertain the possibility that an obstacle that blocks me from effectively using my brain is that I, too, look for sophisticated explanations. But I'm not sure that it is enough to just *tell* myself to think 'simply' and it will happen. There must be psychological barriers that stand in my way of thinking clearly, of thinking like a true scientist.

What I should do is insist that Father show me a practical way to overcome them. But Father doesn't think in terms of psychological barriers, he thinks in terms of external obstacles. He might have a practical way, but even if he has one, how am I going to quickly check if it does overcome my psychological barriers?

At a minimum, I have to have a clear understanding of what those psychological barriers are.

How can I figure that out?

Why not use myself as a guinea pig? I read the document again, this time trying to see what would have blocked me from figuring out his solution, his breakthrough, on my own.

What was his first step? From my experience I know that individuals, and more so groups, have a rather long list of things they are not happy with. He started by cleaning up the mess, by allowing only the important things to remain on the table. Once he brought them to realize the enormous impact that shortages and surpluses have on the net profit, all other things that can be improved took a remote, second place.

I liked the way he explained why they hadn't recognized it before. As a psychologist, I am well aware that people suffering from chronic problems (problems that they already gave up on the possibility of eliminating) develop protective mechanisms. They simply repress these problems.

I'm also aware that people who use those protective mechanisms tend to lower their expectations about life. Simply, since they hide the real problems from themselves, their energy is channeled to deal with the much less important things in their life. So, in spite of their efforts their reality doesn't improve by much; no wonder that after a while they lower their expectations.

It's interesting to me to see that the same thing happens not just with an individual but also with a group, in this case a company. The managers do try to improve their company, but instead of applying all their considerable resources and brainpower to reduce the shortages and the surpluses, most improvement initiatives are channeled to what they allow themselves to see; they are aimed at cost reductions.

Those improvements do yield results, and results accumulate. But as Father pointed out to me more than once, a cent plus a cent plus a cent plus a cent plus a cent plus a cent plus a cent plus a cent plus a cent is still less than a dime. It's no wonder that, as a company, they lowered their expectations; they no longer think that improved operations can bring a tenfold increase to the bottom line.

That's good. Now I know what the first barrier that blocks me is: I too am blind to the big persistent problems, the problems that everybody is camouflaging. Father claims that the obstacle that prevents us from thinking clearly is our distorted perception of reality. It is difficult for me to imagine what change in perception could remove this barrier of mine. So I'll have to carefully check whether or not his suggested perception of reality really helps.

And suppose that I was able to identify the major problems and shut myself away from the noise of the many smaller problems. Would I then be able to come up with the solution?

Obviously not. I continue to read.

Once he got them to concentrate only on the most important phenomena: shortages and surpluses, the core problem was evident—the fact that everything is based on the forecast and the forecast is awful.

I try to imagine how I would continue from that point.

Probably I would try to explore ways to improve the forecast.

The more I think about it the more I'm convinced that I would never say, "Away with using a forecast, let's start from scratch." I would never ask, "How should they operate if their starting assumption was that they didn't know the future demand per item?"

And even if it did cross my mind to contemplate running the operations without a forecast, I'm sure that all the reasons why it cannot be done (the reasons that they naturally raised) would cause me to dismiss this "crazy" idea after no more than a minute or two.

That is my second barrier. What gives *him* the ability

to effortlessly go in such a direction? And stick to it until all the obstacles are removed?

Is it exceptional brainpower? I don't think so. One doesn't need a super brain to say, "Now that we realize that something is awful, can we do without it?" But when this something is at the base, when it is at the foundation of everything that is done, then one needs courage. And, considering the pile of obstacles, that person also needs determination. Father claims that I could have the same abilities if I just abandon the perception that reality is complex. I don't see how a different perception can give a person the needed courage and determination. That is the second thing I'll have to check.

I'm pleased with the progress I'm making. I keep on analyzing his report.

The thing that amazed me, even in my first reading, is that once he reached a wonderful solution, a solution with the potential of delivering the impossible four billion dollars a year, he didn't stop there. He continued to show how it could be extended to achieve much more.

And then he did it again!

I can't visualize me doing the same. I can't visualize anybody else doing it. How many people do I know that once they find a solution, a solution that is capable of reaching the inconceivable, will continue to figure out how to do much better? What gives him the motivation to continue to explore more and more solutions? This ability cannot be described as just courage or determination. Frankly, I am unaware of a proper word for it.

Father's perception of reality must be really effective if it can motivate a person to do such things.

I think I'm ready now. Father, our next meeting will be challenging also for you.

I can't wait for tomorrow.

CHAPTER 4

Inherent Simplicity

Father's expression lights up when I enter his study. But it might be because I'm holding a steaming cup of coffee in my hand. "Thanks, darling," he says as I hand it to him.

"Any new pearls of wisdom from my grandchildren?" he asks.

I first give him the good news. "Amir will be here in two hours to play Heroes with you." Then I cut directly to the chase. "So, can we start? What can help a person to think clearly?"

"Efrat, you know the answer," he replies, and devotes his attention to his coffee.

"Father!"

He leans back in his swivel chair, turns to look directly at me and, smiling, says, "Aren't we full of energy today."

When I make a face, he answers my question. "For a person to think clearly, what is needed is to accept the concept of Inherent Simplicity, not as an interesting speculation, but as the practical way of viewing reality, any reality."

I have frequently heard my father use the phrase Inherent Simplicity. I also realize how central it is to his way of thinking. But frankly, I have never fully understood it.

"Father," I say, "I have been practicing some of your methods for nearly twenty years. I even fool myself that I have added meaningful contributions to the body of knowledge. But, until yesterday, I've treated your teaching as a collection of excellent methods. Not as a way to reach a full life."

"What was so special about yesterday?" he asks.

"For the first time you were talking to me not about methods and applications, but about an approach to life," I answer.

For a while he doesn't reply. Then he says, "Frankly, I don't see much of a difference."

Sometimes Father can be so blind. Rather than arguing I say, "I'd like to fully understand your approach. So, do you mind if I play the devil's advocate while you explain to me what you really mean by Inherent Simplicity?"

"The more devilish you are, the more I'll learn." He grins. "Inherent Simplicity. In a nutshell, it is at the foundation of all modern science as put by Newton: 'Natura valde simplex est et sibi consona.' And, in understandable language, it means, 'nature is exceedingly simple and harmonious with itself.'"

"Can you explain what is meant by exceedingly simple?" I ask.

"Reality usually looks complex to us..."

"That I buy," I interrupt.

He continues, "Take, for example, the movements of all bodies in the world, including collisions and explosions. Can you imagine something more complicated than that?"

Human behavior, I want to say, but I don't want to interrupt him again.

"It looked complex until Newton came up with his three laws of motion. Newton did not invent his three laws, he discovered them. He revealed the Inherent Simplicity that was there. Newton was probably one of the first people to dare to seriously ask the question 'why?' By seriously, I mean to ask why and not be satisfied with an answer that is actually not an answer."

"An answer that's not an answer?"

"For fifteen hundred years before Newton, scientists, like Ptolemy, his teachers and followers, said that the planets are moving in circles. Why? Because a circle is the divine shape. How did they know that circles were the divine shape? Because even the planets are moving in circles.

"Or, why are bodies falling down? Because it is in their nature to fall down. This was the explanation given by Aristotle; an explanation that people accepted as gospel for almost two thousand years. Asking why and insisting on a meaningful answer is the key. Every little kid is a Newton in potential. They relentlessly ask why and they are not happy with answers like 'Go to your mother,' or 'God made it that way.' Remember how Amir defined God? 'The word moms use when they don't know the answer.'"

"I understand the importance of asking why," I say. "But in what way is it connected to the realization that nature is exceedingly simple?"

"Good question. Let me explain how profound Newton's statement is. When we ask why something exists, searching for the cause of that something, we usually get more than one answer or we get an answer that contains more than one component. What will happen if we continue, like a five-year-old, to dive deeper by asking 'why does the cause exist?' in every component of our previous answer? The impression is that we will end up with more and more causes to deal with; the intuitive impression is that systematically using 'why?' will just lead to more and more complexity."

He continues. "What Newton tells us is that the opposite happens; the system converges; common causes appear as we dive down. If we dive deep enough we'll find that there are very few elements at the base—the root causes—which through cause-and-effect connections are governing the whole system. The result of systematically applying the question why is not enormous complexity, but rather wonderful simplicity. Newton had the intuition and the conviction to make the leap of faith that convergence happens, not just for the section of nature he examined in depth, but for any section of nature. Reality is built in wonderful simplicity."

"Wait a minute," I say. "Newton made one leap of faith, but by your last sentence you have added, on top of it, another leap."

"Very observant of you to notice that I substituted the word 'nature' with the word 'reality'." He is apparently pleased. "I'm not talking just about nature; not just about the material world – atoms, electrons, molecules, enzymes. I'm talking about every aspect of reality, including people and whatever they create. The same convergence, the same wonderful simplicity, exists in any aspect of reality. Reality is built in wonderful simplicity."

I have my doubts. Softly I say, "I know that in the hard sciences Newton's speculation is accepted as the foundation; scientists are looking for the root causes without even asking, 'Are we sure that they exist?' But that is not the case in the social sciences. Show me a psychologist who will agree that reality is simple." To provoke him I add, "Don't you know that people are different; that they have the freedom of choice?"

He sighs. "Too many times I've heard the argument that people, unlike the things we deal with in the hard sciences, are not predictable; that people are not subject to cause and effect."

I want to comment, but he gestures that he would like to continue.

"This argument is completely flawed. From firsthand experience I can tell you that I can predict what will happen to me if I'll tell your mother my true opinion of her new car. People are not predictable? Baloney!" In a calmer tone he asks, "Do you accept the statement, 'tell me how you measure me and I'll tell you how I will behave'?"

I remember the first time I heard that sentence. It was when I started to learn psychology, and therefore I investigated it from every possible angle. "You know I do," I answer.

He's on a roll. "Everyone who accepts a statement like this actually admits that people are predictable, that they are subject to cause and effect. In this case the cause is the measurement, and the effect is the resulting behavior. Of course, people are not totally predictable, but neither are electrons. Or the weather. Don't you agree?"

When he turns back to his pipe I say, "You are bursting through an open door. If people were totally unpredictable, there would not be a base for society, or even for family. Moreover, if people were totally unpredictable, I wouldn't have a profession."

"So what is the difference between the material world and the human-based world?" he asks. "Why is it so hard to accept that Inherent Simplicity exists in every part of reality?"

"Because humans are much more complex," I insist. "It's hard for people to accept that Inherent Simplicity exists in what is apparently so complex."

"Efrat," he asks, "are you the same person who talked to me yesterday? Yesterday, you went out of your way to emphasize that a group of people is more complex than an individual and that the most complex cases are organizations. Doesn't the report that I gave you to read clearly show the simple, the embarrassingly simple, root cause that governs a complex organization?" Jokingly he adds, "Maybe that organization was not complex enough for you?"

"Touché," I say, realizing how right he is. A company that deals with the staggering figure of eighty thousand variations is supposed to be complex beyond my imagination. But through his cause-and-effect analysis, through simple common sense logic, he dove down to the root cause and the situation became crystal clear. Clear to the extent that I had to ask myself how come nobody—neither the managers of that company nor the managers of any other apparel company—had realized it before?

I'm still uncomfortable. "On the one hand I am convinced that reality in the case of BigBrand is simple. But I listened to you; I followed your logic; I can even accept whatever you say, and still the fact is that people are complex and BigBrand is an overwhelmingly complex company. How can things that are apparently complex be simple? I don't get it."

He starts to empty his pipe. Then he refills it with tobacco from a small tin box. I wait patiently. When, finally, clouds start to billow out of his mouth, he starts talking. "Suppose that you see two people arguing whether a cucumber is longer or greener. One claims that it is longer because it is green only on the outside but is long both on the outside and on the inside. The other claims that it is greener because it is green for both its length and its width. What do you think, which one of them is right?"

"Father," I say irritatably.

He calmly continues. "The disagreement between these two people doesn't make any sense because 'long' and 'green' are different entities. Maybe you are confused because you are making the same type of mistake?"

"I am not," I firmly say. "A cucumber can be both green and long, but a system cannot be complex and simple at the same time. Simplicity is the opposite of complexity."

"That depends on your definition of complexity," he says. And then he takes a page and draws the following diagrams. "Here are two systems. The one on the left, let's call it system A, is represented by four circles. And the nightmare of circles and arrows on the right is system B. Which of these two systems is more complex?"

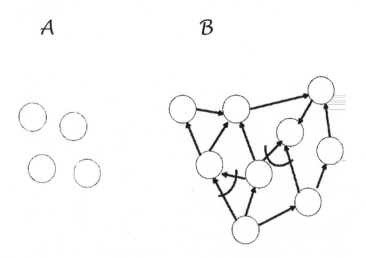

My first inclination is to say that system B is much

more complex. But after thinking for a second, I'm not sure. To be on the safe side I keep my mouth shut.

Father is not bothered by my lack of response. "The answer depends on one's definition of complexity," he starts to explain. "The prevailing definition for complexity is, the more data elements one has to provide in order to fully describe the system, the more complex the system is."

"That's a good definition," I agree. "If one needs only five sentences to describe a system, it is simple, but when one needs hundreds of pages, the system is much more complex."

"According to this definition," he continues, "there is no doubt that system B is much more complex; it contains more circles and, on top of that, it also contains many arrows. And as you probably know, describing a cause-and-effect arrow usually requires more data elements than to describe an entity—a circle."

"Correct," I say. And then smiling I add, "But..."

He smiles back and continues, "But, there is another definition of complexity. If you are a scientist, or a manager, you are not so much interested in the description of the system. You are more interested in the difficulty of controlling and predicting its behavior, especially when changes are introduced. Your definition of complexity is, the more degrees of freedom the system has the more complex it is."

"I'm not a physicist," I remind him. "What do you mean by 'degrees of freedom'?"

"Look at the system and ask yourself, 'what is the minimum number of points you have to touch in order to impact the whole system?' If the answer is one, then the system has only one degree of freedom. That's the case in system B, where if you impact the bottom circle you impact, through the cause-and-effect arrows, every other circle. If the answer is four, as in the case of system A, then the system has four degrees of freedom. By the way, a system that has four degrees of freedom is many orders of magnitude more complex—harder to control and predict—than a system that has only one degree of freedom. Now Efrat, what is your answer? Which system, A or B, is more complex?"

Slowly I say, "The answer depends on the definition of complexity." I'm still trying to digest. "So, BigBrand is overwhelmingly complex according to the first definition. But when we succeed in building the causes and effects and we find that there is only one entity at the bottom—only one root cause—we realize that it is extremely simple. And yes, as a result of this understanding we now know how it will react to changes, including the change that could propel its bottom line performance into new records."

Then I add, "I need some time to adjust to the fact that people and organizations can be incredibly complex and still be exceedingly simple. That complexity and simplicity can coexist. One thing is clear; this concept of Inherent Simplicity is much more powerful than I thought."

"We haven't finished," he grins. "So far, we've discussed just one obstacle that blocks people from effectively using their brainpower—the perception that reality is complex. The concept of Inherent Simplicity helps us to remove not just the first obstacle but also the second obstacle."

"What is the second obstacle?"

He looks at me thoughtfully for a moment and then says, "Efrat, if you don't mind, I think that it will be better if I continue by explaining Newton's statement—explaining the other aspect of Inherent Simplicity. It will enable you to not only identify the second obstacle but also to realize the extent to which overcoming it helps pave the way to a full life."

"I'm all ears."

"Unfortunately," he says, "it will take some time, and darling, there is something much more important I would like to do now." And he turns to his computer to bring up Heroes; his grandchild will be back soon.

CHAPTER 5

Contradictions and Conflicts

While they are playing, I try to articulate my deeper understanding of what he calls Inherent Simplicity.

He talks about what is actually there, not on the surface, but right below it. He talks about what does exist if we just bother to scratch the surface.

If we break a situation down to its finer and finer components; if we allow ourselves to be immersed in the immense number of details describing these components and the relationships between them, then we'll just end up with a bigger and bigger appreciation of the situation's complexity.

This is also correct when we examine the relationship between any two closely related people. Just listen to them when they describe the history of their relationship; a mother and her teenage daughter, two friends, a person and his counterpart at work, not to mention a married couple. Very soon you'll get tired of listening to the vast details and to the inconsistencies between the stories.

It is even more correct, more complex, when one person is the subject, since every person has relationships with many different people. Of course, when we examine an organization, an entity that is composed of many different people, the complexity is overwhelming.

The claim is that in all these situations there is Inherent Simplicity. The simplicity will emerge when all those numerous components and all those immense details are all connected through simple cause-and-effect relationships, and when they all stem from just a very few elements. That was Newton's belief about nature. That is Father's belief about reality.

He doesn't claim that reality is not overwhelmingly complex; he acknowledges it in full. But what he says is that there is a way to realize that, from another more important aspect, it is exceedingly simple.

Do I accept that?

As long as it is just a philosophical speculation I really don't care. But, if Father does convince me that it helps to think like a true scientist, then it is a different story. I want to live a full life and I am aware that clear thinking helps to achieve it. What I must clarify is whether or not the belief in Inherent Simplicity will help me to overcome the barriers that block me from thinking clearly. Last night I identified three such barriers. But first I have to fully understand the other part of this strange concept of Inherent Simplicity. I wait impatiently for them to finish playing that stupid computer game.

Once my mother forces Amir to go eat, and Father squeezes a kiss from him, I get his full attention.

Leaning back, he picks up right where we left off. "So far we have dealt with the first half of Newton's statement. The latter part of his statement, the one that states that nature is harmonious with itself, is not less important."

"Harmonious with itself," I repeat. "How should I interpret such a phrase?"

"One interpretation might be that there are no contradictions," he explains.

"What's so important about that?" I ask. "Isn't it obvious that nature doesn't contain contradictions?"

"Okay, my smart daughter, let me rephrase Newton's sentence to be: reality does not contain conflicts. Would you accept it now? Remember, human beings are part of reality."

He just gave me the key. Triumphantly, I say, "That's the difference between the material world and the human-based world—between the hard sciences and the soft sciences. The material world does not contain contradictions. But people have conflicts, not just between each other—every person is struggling with internal conflicts."

"There is another way to look at it," he says.

That's too much. "Father, I can assure you that there is no way you can convince me that people don't have conflicts."

He resorts to his pipe.

After a while he starts again. "Let me take a step back. Maybe we should discuss the differences and similarities between the words contradiction and conflict."

Since I don't know where he is heading I keep quiet.

"Let's examine an example of how deep everybody's conviction is that there are no contradictions in the material world. Suppose that we have two different techniques to measure the height of a building. And when we use them to measure the height of a specific building we get two very different heights. Facing such an apparent contradiction no one would say, let's compromise; let's agree that the height of this building is the average between the two measurements.

"What we would say is that somewhere along the line we have made an erroneous assumption. We'll check to see if, in the time that passed between the two measurements, additional floors were added. If that's not the case, we'll explore if our assumption—that each of the measurements was carried out properly—is correct. If they were, we'll look for an erroneous assumption in the techniques themselves; we'll explore the possibility that one of these two techniques is faulty. In extreme cases we'll even doubt our understanding of height. But we'll always look for the erroneous assumption and never contemplate the possibility of compromise. This is how strong our belief is that there are no contradictions in nature."

I'm not impressed. "A building cannot have two different heights, that's obvious. But a person can have two conflicting desires."

"Believe me, I know," he says. "I know that people may have conflicts. But that is also the situation in the material world. It is filled with conflicts. Reality doesn't contain contradictions, but it is full of conflicts.

"Can you explain the difference between a contradiction and a conflict?"

"Conflict is a situation where we want a contradiction." When he sees that doesn't help, he hurries to explain. "Take, for example, the wing of an airplane. On one hand, we need the wings to be strong. And in order to ensure the strength we should use thick supporting beams. But on the other hand, we need the wings to be light, and in order to ensure *that*, we should use thin supporting beams. A typical conflict. And like any other conflict, including conflicts between people, it will lead in good situations to some acceptable compromise, and in bad situations to a stone wall."

"Actually," I say, "in many situations a conflict will lead to a bad compromise. To a compromise that is bad because it is the cause of many undesirable effects. Come to think of it, I cannot think of even one example of an undesirable effect that is not the result of a conflict."

"No argument," he agrees. "What I'm suggesting is that we treat any conflict like a scientist treats a contradiction."

In the last ten years I've gained a lot of experience, most of it successful, in using his conflict removal method. So I allow myself to take over. "In other words," I say, "when we face a conflict, especially when we cannot easily find an acceptable compromise, let's do exactly the same thing we do when we encounter a contradiction; let's insist that one of the underlying assumptions is faulty. If, or should I say when, we pin down the underlying assumption that can be removed, we remove the cause of the conflict; we solve the conflict by eliminating it."

"Correct," he says. "So can you now verbalize the second obstacle that prevents people from effectively using their brainpower?"

Slowly I say, "I need a minute to organize my thoughts."

Yesterday I came to the conclusion that meaningful opportunities are open when one sees how to remove a blockage; how to overcome an undesirable situation that I'm convinced I cannot change. Many times, the blockage is due to a conflict that does not have an acceptable compromise. From experience I know that as long as we think that the only way to handle a conflict is by compromising, we'll never think about the underlying assumptions and how to remove at least one of them; we'll never find the way to eliminate the conflict; we'll never come up with the breakthrough; we'll never reveal the great opportunity that hides there. We'll just lower our expectations.

Confidently I say, "The second obstacle is that people's perception is that conflicts are a given and that the best we can do is to seek a compromise."

Bitterly Father remarks, "In academia we are encouraging that devastating mistake. Under the glorifying title of 'optimization' we invest considerable efforts to teach students, not how to remove conflicts, but how to waste time finding the 'best' compromise. What a waste of talent."

"Can you summarize Inherent Simplicity for me?" I ask, to keep him from getting sidetracked talking about the problems of education.

"What I mean by Inherent Simplicity is that reality, any part of reality, is governed by very few elements, and that any existing conflict can be eliminated." And then he adds, "If we take that as a given, as absolutely correct in every situation, we'll find ourselves thinking clearly." And he turns to refill his pipe.

I haven't finished yet. "Let's put it to the test. Can you explain to me how your belief in Inherent Simplicity helped with the BigBrand case?"

"Isn't it too late to start that discussion now?"

"It is. See you tomorrow." I go upstairs to collect the kids.

CHAPTER 6

Putting the
Belief to Work

I deliver the kids to their schools and head directly to my parents' house. When I arrive, Father is still fast asleep. I tiptoe into his bedroom. He makes a sound. "Let's put your belief in Inherent Simplicity to the test," I whisper.

"Efrat," he groans, "you are as ferocious as your mother." But less than ten minutes later he enters his study. "Where is my coffee?" he growls.

I hand it to him. Then I hand him his pipe and wait for him to light it.

When I see that he is comfortable, I start. "I went over the BigBrand report and I'm convinced that on my own I would never have been able to come up with such a nice analysis and solution. So either you admit that I don't have enough brainpower or you demonstrate to me how the belief in Inherent Simplicity can help me to think like a true scientist.?

"Hmm…" is his only response.

I don't give up. "For example, I want to understand how your belief in Inherent Simplicity helped you to concentrate on the effects that everybody else is camouflaging; on the 'sold-outs' and the 'end-of-season sales'."

"Efrat," he says, "I didn't bother to do a full analysis of BigBrand. It would have taken too much time. I tried to find a way to significantly improve its performance, and that's the reason I was examining only a fraction of that company. Since it is a very good company, most things are working well. I was examining just what doesn't work well; I concentrated on the undesirable effects."

"That's important." I make a mental note to myself. "And..."

He continues, "Because of my belief in Inherent Simplicity, I took for granted that the whole section, all the things that do not work well, are caused by very few elements. Actually, from my experience, I expected just one element; one root cause. Also, since I was dealing with undesirable effects I took for granted that the root cause is a conflict that doesn't have an acceptable compromise. I took for granted that the undesirable effects are the outcome of an unsatisfactory compromise."

I think about it. Aloud. "People tend to repress chronic problems, problems that they have given up on the possibility of solving. Your belief in Inherent Simplicity caused you to take for granted that these problems can be solved because they are the result of a root conflict and that the conflict can be removed. That's why you didn't have a tendency to camouflage these problems. I see."

"Moreover," I continue, "the smaller problems are those that can be disconnected from the compromise, and that's the reason they can be handled while the conflict stays intact. So starting with a small problem cannot guarantee that it will lead you to the root conflict. But your target was to zoom in on the root conflict. So not only were you not repressing the chronic problems, you were eagerly looking for them."

"Whatever you say, dear," he sighs. "When I'm trying to improve a situation, I simply don't see much point wasting time on small problems when I can solve the big ones. Much more return for basically the same effort."

I like my explanation much better than his. It explains how Inherent Simplicity helps to overcome the first psychological barrier, the tendency to camouflage the big problems. What about the courage and determination to look for a daring solution; a solution like replacing the forecast as the base for operations?

It is so obvious now. I'm sure that if I had told him that he needed courage and determination he would have laughed in my face. The belief in Inherent Simplicity is all he needed. Part of the belief in Inherent Simplicity is that any conflict, including root conflicts, can be removed by removing one of the underlying false assumptions. That's what he has done. That is what he intended to do even before he knew the specific conflict and the specific underlying assumption.

Therefore he first identified the root conflict—order more to avoid shortages versus order less to avoid surpluses. Then he identified the underlying assumption—the only way to order the correct quantity is to know what the demand will be in advance; in other words, to forecast the demand. Then, his natural reaction was to try and replace the underlying assumption. To ask, "How should they operate if their starting assumption is that they do not know the future demand per item?" It is also no wonder, that in spite of all the obstacles, he persisted, because his belief in Inherent Simplicity assured him that he was on the right path. It's powerful.

Actually, that is what I'm doing with my clients. They come to me not because everything is nice and dandy but because they have problems; they have undesirable effects. Since I've started using Father's techniques I, too, assume, a priori, that the undesirable effects they complain about are the result of a conflict—a conflict between the parties in cases of relationships, and an internal conflict in cases of individuals. Once I properly verbalize the core conflict, I, too, expose the underlying assumptions and try to guide them to realize that there are ways to replace those assumptions.

Maybe the only difference between individuals and organizations is that in cases of organizations the underlying assumptions are perceived not as assumptions but as facts of life. And therefore it is more difficult to identify and challenge them. Or maybe the only difference is in my head; I feel comfortable dealing with individuals but I feel less competent dealing with organizations.

I look at my watch. Soon I have to go pick up the boys. But I still have to find out about the third psychological barrier. Why didn't he stop when he found an excellent solution?

"Why did you continue to look for better and better solutions?" I ask as I stand up.

"Actually, I didn't," he confesses. "But I did change an underlying assumption so I felt compelled to see all the ramifications; to complete the full picture of my new understanding of reality. The fact that two additional enhancements emerged was a side effect, a somewhat expected side effect. Reality is built in wonderful simplicity and I enjoy seeing wonderful things."

I give him a hug.

As we walk to the car I thank him. "At last I think I understand what you mean by Inherent Simplicity."

"Not yet darling. An important angle is still missing."

CHAPTER 7

Harmony

Father doesn't look surprised when, two hours later, I'm back in his study. "What am I missing?" I ask.

He knows exactly what I'm asking for. Without any hesitation he answers, "Newton said 'nature is exceedingly simple and harmonious with itself.' I think that reducing the interpretation of 'harmonious with itself' to just 'doesn't contain contradictions' is missing the real beauty of the harmony that exists in nature. Every scientist who has contributed something meaningful to our understanding commented with awe on that harmony."

I am a pragmatic person. What I like about Father's way of thinking is that everything is clearly explained. First, the basic assumptions are explicitly spelled out. Then, using airtight logic, the technique is derived. Finally, it is all summarized by a list of instructions, which are few and easy to follow. To hear him talking about intangible mischief like awe of harmony makes me uneasy.

"This is what I rushed to come back for?" I cannot hide my disappointment.

He tries to explain. "You see, it's amazing how frequently things that seem to be unrelated are connected to form a bigger picture. Similarities and symmetries emerge out of nowhere with such frequency that scientists start to expect and use it. Harmony is everywhere."

When he realizes that I'm still uncomfortable, he wonders aloud, "How can I expose you to that sensation?"

"Is it important?" I sigh. "I mean, will it help me to think more clearly?"

"Okay, let's take it one step at a time. We already covered the first two obstacles to thinking clearly—the perception that reality is complex, and the tendency to accept conflicts as a given. What if I tell you that deeper understanding of the extent to which reality is harmonious helps a lot in overcoming the third obstacle that stands in the way of thinking clearly? And darling, don't fool yourself; you, too, are blocked by that obstacle."

"That's interesting. What's the third obstacle?" I ask.

"Before answering, I need to ask you something."

"Go ahead."

"Let me speculate that you, like any other person, have been involved in relationships that were far from harmonious. Can you tell me what you think were the reasons for the disharmony?"

I rush a few such relationships through my mind before I answer. "It is because the people I had the relationships with were too egotistical. They were looking mainly after their own interests and didn't care much how their demands affected me."

Since he doesn't ask further I say, "Now can you tell me what the third obstacle is?"

"The third obstacle is that we tend to blame the other party." Smiling he adds, "Exactly like you just did."

I cannot stop myself from commenting, "It's not that I'm blaming. I'm just stating the facts." And then I ask, "In what way is blaming an obstacle?"

"Blaming another person is not a solution…"

I interject, "But it does point in the direction of the solution."

"That is exactly the problem," he says. "In too many cases blaming points us in the wrong direction, into a direction where we will not find a good solution. Even if the person will be removed, in most cases the problem will stay."

I check several such scenarios in my mind to verify if he is right. He might be.

"Moreover," he continues, "blaming others pours fuel onto the fire. It is a recipe to ruin the harmony in the relationship."

"That I buy," I smile.

"Efrat, thinking clearly also means finding the most effective path toward your target. In this sense knowing how to preserve harmony in relationships is extremely important for a person who wants to live a full life. Whenever you go after promising opportunities, you will probably need a lot of collaboration from other people. If the relationships are not harmonious you cannot expect to get good collaboration, and the chances of bringing an important opportunity to fruition will be severely reduced."

"And if the other party is at fault?" I ask. And then I add, "I'll just have to carefully choose the people I will work with… But that's not always possible. Okay, continue. But now I need to know what you recommend instead of blaming."

"That brings us back to the importance of the conviction that reality is harmonious. Shall we first check what the definition of harmony is?" he suggests.

When he stands up to look for a dictionary I sit down in his place to search the Internet.

In the Oxford dictionary I find (after ignoring, without

Father's consent, the definitions that relate to music) the following definitions: "The quality of forming a pleasing and consistent whole," and "Agreement or concord." In Webster's dictionary the definitions are: "Compatibility in opinion and action," and "Agreement of opinions."

These definitions match my understanding of harmony.

"How can the concept of harmony help me to stop blaming people?" I ask. And to myself I think, "Why shouldn't I blame people when they are at fault?"

"Can I have my chair back?" he asks. He takes his time refilling his pipe. Then he spends three matches until he is satisfied that it burns well. At last he addresses my question. "You will be able to refrain from blaming people when you are convinced there is no reason to blame them. And before you jump to the conclusion that I'm talking about a utopian world, let me highlight that the belief in Inherent Simplicity also implies a deep conviction that harmony exists in any relationship between people." Smiling, he waits for my reaction.

As he expects I cannot hold back my surprise. "Harmony exists in any relationship between people? Are you serious?"

His smile broadens. "Pay attention, Daughter. I didn't say that every relationship is harmonious. I'm well aware that harmonious relationships are rare; much too rare."

"Harmony exists in any relationship, nevertheless most relationships are not harmonious? I'm totally confused."

"What I'm claiming is that while harmony does exist in any relationship between people, unfortunately in most cases we don't bother to find and actually implement it."

Seeing that I'm lost he suggests, "Maybe an example will help. To demonstrate what I mean, why don't you give me a case where you are convinced that the relationship is not harmonious and is likely to continue to deteriorate. And I'll prove to you that, right below the surface, everything is already there to foster a harmonious relationship. But for the example to be helpful please choose a generic case rather than giving me a specific, convoluted story."

I wouldn't have any problem giving him specific cases. The first that comes to mind is my friend who is going through a nasty divorce. But he is right, to describe the situation I'd have to dive into details and he could use each detail to claim that a different behavior would lead to a better relationship. That will lead us nowhere. It is much better to bring up a generic case where it is obvious that no harmonious relationship is likely. It will be fun to see him struggle, and fail, with the impossible task of proving that everything is already there to turn it into a harmonious relationship.

"Give me a minute," I say.

I try to visualize hypothetical scenes of two parties who have a close relationship: a mother and a teenage daughter; a married couple; a manager and his counterpart. Of course for each type I can bring cases of bad relationships, even extremely bad relationships, but overall, in most of these cases relationships are quite good. In spite of occasional disputes, almost all mothers and daughters love each other dearly. Most married couples that do stay together do so not because it is too difficult to get a divorce, but because they want to continue to be together. Between most associates there is camaraderie. I'll have to approach it from a different angle.

What are the characteristics of situations where I expect inharmonious relationships? I'll certainly find an inharmonious relationship when the relationship is not typified by camaraderie and loyalty but by gripes and complaints. When there is a big asymmetry between the two parties; one party is almost totally dependent on the other while the other has plenty of equivalent alternatives.

The problem is that many times the strong party pretends that the relationship is fine; they turn a blind eye to the animosity they cause in the other party.

What are the scenarios where it is almost impossible to hide the fact that the relationships are far from being harmonious?

I know. It is when one party, because of its selfish interests, demands a major change from the other party.

When is such a demand likely to appear?

Suppose that one party is doing an analysis concentrating on the changes needed to increase its own benefits. If the analysis is thorough and the resulting benefits are big, it stands to reason that the required changes are fundamental changes in the mode of operation. It also stands to reason that to reach the benefits, a change is also required from the other related party. Naturally, the party that did the analysis has major concerns when it approaches the other party and asks it to agree to make the required change. From my experience I know that when the required changes are fundamental, I expect the other party to raise some objections; if the relationship was not good to start with, I expect that the initial response will be negative, even nasty.

I have the perfect generic example that fits the above like a glove. It is the relationship between most large companies and their small, run-of-the-mill suppliers. And I know the exact scenario where Father will find that it is impossible to find a way to foster harmony. It is when the true nature of the relationship is revealed;

when the large company comes up with yet another demand on the small supplier.

"Father," I say sweetly, "can you tell me the concerns of the managers at BigBrand regarding the solution you unfolded to them?"

He thinks about it for a little while before answering. "Strangely enough, the thing that concerned them the most was how difficult and time-consuming it would be to persuade their contractors to collaborate; that a high level of dictation, resulting in more bad blood, would be needed to convince the contractors to change their mode of operation."

That is exactly what I expected. In the same sweet voice I say, "Father, that is the example that I want. Show me what harmony exists between a brand company and a contractor in this case."

He looks at me with appreciation. "You are a tough cookie."

I just smile.

He releases another cloud of smoke. "You expect the contractor to resist the request, actually the demand, to switch from the tradition of getting large orders enough time in advance, to the frantic mode of quick response to small orders. It is reasonable to expect resistance."

"Reasonable?" I don't accept such an understatement. "Look at it from the contractor's point of view. Put yourself in the shoes of the managers of a small contractor. Facing such a selfish demand from the brand company, wouldn't you be frustrated and bitter? Wouldn't you blame the brand company for being a selfish bully?"

Turning to his computer he says, "The report that I'm about to send you is exactly what you just asked for; it is looking at the same situation, but from the point of view of a contractor. Sweetheart, prepare yourself for a major surprise."

CHAPTER 8

Never Say "I Know"*

When coming to evaluate the applicability of our generic solution to a specific case, there is a rule that I am trying to stick to—check and crosscheck if our assumptions about the key data on which our suggested solution is based are valid for the specific case. Recently, I had to face a case where it was apparent that I had deviated from that rule. Of course, the consequences were embarrassing, but that is not the reason I'm now forcing myself to sit down and write this document. I'm not a masochist. The main reason is that the renewed analysis showed me, again, the extent to which there is no end to deeper understanding; we have embarked on a journey that does not have an end, just exciting and rewarding stepping stones.

Maybe I was "hit" by this case because the company is

---

*This report was written and circulated to the Goldratt Group in May 2006. For the purpose of this book it was slightly modified to enable easy reading for readers who are not familiar with the Theory of Constraints.

producing sporting apparel. If there is a sector that I fooled myself I knew inside and out, it is manufacturing-based companies. Nevertheless, the renewed analysis yielded not one, but three additions to the body of knowledge. The importance of these additions can be evaluated by the fact that in the following few weeks I used them effectively for two other consumer goods manufacturers.

Here are the details. Eighty-five percent of the company's income comes from being a contractor to the big brand companies.

Usually, a contractor will have one or two dominant clients. A dominant client has the power to squeeze a low price from its contractors. Low prices translate into low gross margins, purchased materials being a high percentage of income. But this company has over ten brand companies as clients, none of them dominating its sales. Therefore I wasn't overly surprised when I was told that their material cost is only half of their income.

The other fifteen percent of sales come from their own collection, their own brand, which they sell through their own ten shops and a few more franchised shops, all located in their small country.

A textbook case. In the first meeting I verified that their production lead time is two months (very common in the apparel industry) and yes, they produce for the entire season in one batch and ship it before the beginning of the season to the brand companies.

This company is located in Europe. So, relative to their competitors in the Far East they do have a big advantage that they are not using today: transportation time to the central warehouses of all their clients is only a few days. This proximity to the markets is wasted since their long production lead time puts them at two months distance from their clients. But there is no real setup in production of sports apparel, so it should be easy to cut the lead time to less than a week. About twenty-five years ago I published the relevant knowledge, and since then it has been implemented in hundreds of such plants.

To turn their advantage into a real competitive edge one just has to realize the eagerness of the brand companies to reduce their inventories. What the brands love, almost to the extent that they like to further reduce the price they pay to the contractor, is that the contractor will hold the inventory for them. The contractor's proximity, coupled with drastically shorter production lead times, will enable them to provide this service for just a modest increase in cost.

Offering this service, the contractor will be able to get as many orders as they are able to handle. And they will be able to handle much more than today since a side effect of reducing the production lead time is the exposure of significant excess capacity, enough to support almost doubling sales without increasing manpower.

To support more than double the current sales, the contractor will need to increase capacity. That is not a problem; there is no shortage of people to sew, and the machines are just sewing machines. With material cost as low as just half the selling price, bringing their profit to be equal to their current sales will necessitate just an increase in direct labor by about fifty percent.

Next case please.

During the preliminary extensive checks with management it turned out that a key data element was wrong—material cost is not fity percent of sales, rather it is seventy-five percent. Even when the big brand companies are not dominant clients, they have the power to squeeze low prices from a contractor that is too eager to grow fast. Gross margins that are so small change the entire picture; to bring the company to excellent profits it is not enough just to increase sales, they must significantly increase margins as well. In short, kiss good-bye a vision based on just holding the inventories for the brand companies.

Two different questions should be answered. To avoid running again into such an embarrassment we need to know why such a basic piece of data was wrong. And, to ensure that we do have a vision for contractors that supply to brands, we should also try and answer a more interesting question. Is there a feasible way to increase margins?

As for the first question, it didn't take long to reveal the source of the mistake. The fifty percent was derived from their financial statements. Therefore, it represents an average over their two channels of sales. Even though the other channel—direct sales through their own shops—is relatively small (just fifteen percent), it had a major impact on the average percentage of material. Simply put, for the channel of direct sales, the material represents much, much less than fifty percent of the selling price (margins in the direct sales channel are composed of the huge markup of their own brand plus the substantial markup of their own shops).

We now understand the source of the mistake. But it doesn't help us to answer the much more interesting question. What can we do to increase margins?

Asking for a premium price for rapid response is the first thing that jumps to mind, especially when one considers the current production lead time of two months and the ease of cutting the production lead time to be, at most, one week. Well, in their environment there is a limitation that makes it difficult. Dying the fabric is a batch process. Therefore, their suppliers will be reluctant to dye small quantities. Moreover, the suppliers are not willing to guarantee the same color in subsequent batches.

Knowing the amazing benefits that moving from producing to meet the forecast to producing for actual consumption brings the brand companies, I first concentrated on finding a way to solve the problem of the need for large batches of dyed fabric.

Suppose that all garments are produced from just one dyed fabric. What would happen if the company buys the material in large quantities, but produces—converts the materials to garments—in small quantities as dictated by actual consumption? True, like today, the investment in material would occur much earlier than consumption, but real gain would eventually be achieved. There would be almost no shortages or surpluses of garments.

Since all garments are not produced from just one dyed fabric, the extent to which such a mode of operation will be effective in reducing shortages and surpluses depends on the extent to which the same fabric is used for different garments.

We all know that to some extent the same dyed fabric is used for different garments since all sizes of the same model use exactly the same dyed fabric. Unfortunately, this cannot help much. In fashion the forecast is particularly lousy because the lifetime of the products in the market is too short. Consumption data that has been collected in one season cannot be used for forecasting the next season's consumption because the products are different. But that is not the case for forecasting the relative consumption of the different sizes; the ratio between consumption of a large size and a small size tends to stay the same for years.

So it all depends on the extent to which the same dyed fabric is used for different models. For that I checked the number of different models they produce per year (35,000) and compared it to the number of different dyed fabrics they use per year (4,700). The ratio is one to seven. Is it enough?

We know that, in general, about thirty percent of the SKUs suffer from shortages—they are depleted before the massive end-of-the-season clearance sales start. They are the high runners. Another thirty percent suffer from surpluses—they are sold mainly in the end-of-the-season sales and in the outlets. They are the slow movers. That means that in a group of seven models there is a high chance, over ninety percent, that at least one model will be a high runner, while at least one other model will be a slow mover. So even though we start with a given (forecasted) amount of dyed fabric, still, in most cases, the diversion that we can do (from the actual slow movers to the actual high runners) will help. But *how much* will it help?

To answer this question we have to realize the nonlinear nature of the damage shortages cause. Suppose the season lasts four months and that a particular item has been depleted after one month. How much are the lost sales relative to the amount that was sold? One doesn't have to be a trained mathematician to answer this question. The lost sales are three times bigger than the actual sales. What about an item that is completely sold out after three months? The lost sales are just one third of the actual sales (less, if one takes into account that in the last month of the season prices are lower). This means that even though we work with restricted availability of the colored fabric, we can get most of the effect, in terms of percent increase in sales, since most lost sales can be prevented. The same goes for reducing the bad effect of surpluses, especially when we consider that the longer it takes until the slow mover is sold, the lower the price at which it is sold.

How can we take advantage of it? How can we turn it into a mafia offer (an offer they can't refuse) for the brand companies? Currently the brand companies order the amount needed for the whole season and demand delivery before the beginning of the season. Once they get the goods they immediately push about forty percent into retail to fill up the pipelines with the new collection. Let's not try to change these big companies. Let's give them an offer that does not require any real change on their side, and one in which the advantages of our offer will be apparent to them.

What do you think about the following offer? Continuing to follow the current practice, the contractor will get the orders per item, based on forecast, in enough time before the beginning of the season. Based on the orders, the contractor buys the entire quantity of dyed fabric, as it currently does. But the contractor will cut, sew and ship only half the forecasted quantity of each item (the quantity needed to fill the pipelines in retail and leave some spare at the brand warehouses). Now the contractor waits for the orders to come to the brand company from the retailers. The first orders are apparently orders for high runners. The contractor is informed of each order that the brand gets, and as long as it still has that dyed fabric, it will replenish within a time period that is very short relative to the period of the season; two weeks should be enough for a system that is used to a minimum of two months. Six weeks before the end of the season, the brand should instruct the contractor what should be done with any residual fabric. Should it be turned into garments or should it be held for the next year (at the brand's expense)? I think that if such an offer is presented well, with a full explanation of the benefits the brand will unavoidably gain, the chances are very high that each and every brand will gladly accept.

As a matter of fact, knowing that all brands are currently struggling to find ways to increase their inventory turns, I think that they will be interested in such an offer to the extent that the contractor can use it effectively to increase its margins. Here I'm going into the speculative mode; the following should be checked with the brands and modified according to their response.*

---

*Within one year of writing this report, such an offer was presented to several brands. They all accepted it with open arms.

Brands that operate on three seasons a year (the standard in sports apparel) have about six inventory turns. For them, increasing to nine inventory turns is a major achievement. I doubt that anyone in those companies thinks that twelve inventory turns is realistic for the company. Therefore, requesting a bonus based on actual inventory turns might fly. The contractor should present his offer along the lines of:

> Right now, in sporting apparel, you have six inventory turns. With our offer, which is based on the mammoth efforts that we have made to improve our reaction time from over two months to less than two weeks (including transportation), we think you can achieve higher inventory turns. Let's take the conservative assumption that fluctuations (and a lot of luck) might bring your inventory turns on our goods to eight. So, let's acknowledge our contribution to your improved results only if your inventory turns go up to the delightful number of nine. But then, compensate us for our unique contribution. For example, for each inventory turn starting at nine, give us a bonus equal to just five percent of our price.

Since the markup on the brands is usually around four hundred percent of the price they pay to their contractors and since increasing their inventory turns is of such importance to them, such an offer has a real chance of being accepted, at least by three or four of the twelve clients the company has. Of course, to conclude such a deal we'll have to climb the ladder, from the purchasing agent to a relatively high-level manager, so don't expect a quick deal.

What impact will it have on the contractor's margins? My founded expectation is that such an offer will actually bring the inventory turns of a brand (without any action from the brand to change the way it does business with the retailer) from six to fifteen turns.* The offer has the potential to double the contractor's margins while dramatically increasing its sales.

I have some slight hesitations. Simply, we haven't yet tried having the brand give bonuses for improved inventory turns, or anything similar. So I kept on thinking about additional ways, to be done in parallel, to increase the company's margins while dramatically increasing their sales.

How can they get higher margins? I couldn't think of an additional way to get a higher price from the company's clients—the brand companies. So what about...

---

*At first glance, fifteen inventory turns seems optimistic, but actually it is very conservative. Just consider that right after the beginning of a season a brand currently holds 60% (40% are shipped almost immediately to retail) of the goods (this number decreases slowly during the season), while using our way the brand will hold just 10% of the goods. So we can expect that the inventory turns will increase five-fold, and that is without taking into account that sales will go up due to fewer shortages of the high runners. Fifteen inventory turns is very conservative.

CHAPTER 9

Win-Win

I stop reading Father's report because my mind is racing.

Before reading it, I was absolutely sure that the contractors would resent the demand of BigBrand; the demand to switch from the tradition of getting large orders enough time in advance, to the much more demanding mode of quick response to small orders. I blamed the brand for demanding something that is unfair. I was convinced that this demand would be bad for the contractors. I hadn't taken the time to examine how it would affect the contractors' operations, and nevertheless I assumed that it was bad. Why did I jump to this conclusion?

I assumed that it would be bad because this demand stemmed from a selfish analysis—an analysis aimed at increasing the benefits of BigBrand—and did not consider the needs and interests of the contractors. In other words, I took for granted that if one party concentrates on its selfish benefits (especially when that party is strong and dominant) the result must be a change that is bad for the other parties.

What I had just read woke me up to the possibility that this preconceived notion might not be right. Not only is the change not necessarily bad for the other party, it might be good. Good to the extent that when the contractor does its own selfish analysis it might come up with, basically, the same change that BigBrand would propose.

Now I begin to realize what Father means when he claims that harmony exists in any relationship. Certainly he doesn't fool himself by thinking that every relationship is harmonious, but what he claims is that for every relationship there is a change that will cause the parties to each achieve what they need from the relationship. And when all parties want the same change, "compatibility in opinion and action exists." Harmony exists by definition. When Father says that harmony exists, he means that it is possible to construct such a change now, even though the change might not have been recognized yet and therefore the current relationship is far from being harmonious.

Of course, considering the contractor's current perception about the brands—considering that a contractor expects to get from a brand only new selfish demands—even a suggested change that is good for both parties has to be presented carefully.

I'm trying to envision what the contractor's reaction will be if the brand will first acknowledge the contractor's need; will acknowledge that the contractor will benefit from higher income. I don't see how the contractor can object to it, and I don't think that any contractor will fool itself that the brand, all of a sudden, became philanthropic. Most likely the contractor will suspiciously wait for the other shoe to drop—for the accompanying conditions.

Then suppose that the brand states that it is willing to contemplate paying higher prices if, and only if, a change will be instituted—a change that will enable the brand to enjoy considerably higher inventory turns. I think that with an introduction like that the contractor will be open to seriously examining the proposed change. And once the contractor realizes that such a change can be implemented—that his cost will not be adversely impacted; that the brand is willing to implement its side of the change and the result is likely to increase the contractor's margin—once these points are understood the collaboration is very likely. And even if a gentle, or less than gentle, push is required, once the contractor gets the higher prices his appreciation of the brand and his willingness to continue to strengthen the relationship with the brand will certainly get a big boost.

Of course, many contractors will try to squeeze a little more; a higher increase in price than the brand initially offers. But the change brings such huge benefits to the brand that it can afford to be flexible.

The key is: "A change that will bring the parties to each achieve what they need from the relationship." Introducing such a change to a situation that is currently a mess will open exciting opportunities. And once the parties realize that this change enables each of them to achieve what they want, it will not be too difficult to implement it. If Father is right, that such changes can exist for any relationship, it is not just helpful, it is the key for reaching a full life.

But how does one go about uncovering that magnificent change? Even if it exists, one needs an exceptional, innovative mind to come up with it. I don't fool myself that I have the phenomenal intuition to come up with the right hunch, or the brainpower needed to turn that hunch into a well-thought-out change. Is this the end of the road for me? Should I give up?

Father claims that everyone, including me, has enough intuition and brainpower. Easy for him to say.

He claims that the real problem is not lack of intuition and brainpower, but that we block ourselves from using what we have by our tendency to blame others. Isn't that what he demonstrated with this report? Here I am giving him the most difficult scenario I could think of; a scenario where I was convinced that nobody would be able to find even a trace of harmony, and what did he force me to realize? In that scenario my problem was not to find the change, the "magnificent" change was known to me: to switch from the tradition of large orders based on forecast to the mode of quick response based on actual consumption. I knew the required change, but it didn't cross my mind that it would enable both parties to get what each wants. I was blocked by the fact that I, a priori, blamed the brand company for demanding an unfair change.

I start to accept that Father is right; I was blinded by my mind-set—the mind-set that the demand from the big company must be bad for the other party—the mind-set of blaming.

Father is talking about three different obstacles. The first one is the obstacle of viewing reality as complex, and the second is accepting conflicts as given. These two obstacles are preventing people from coming up with the required change. I'm about to accept that if I become proficient in utilizing the fact that even seemingly complex situations are governed by common sense cause-and-effect logic, I will be able to more and more quickly zoom in on the core conflict. At least in cases where I do have enough intuition and knowledge. I'm also ready to accept that once the core conflict is clearly verbalized I'll not take it as a given; I'll find the assumption that should be removed. In other words, there is a real chance that I'll be able to find the direction of the magnificent change.

Now I see why Father insisted that I acknowledge the third obstacle: the tendency to blame. As long as I do not overcome this tendency, even when the change is presented to me on a golden platter, I'll ignore it. What a lesson. Father said, "Sweetheart, prepare yourself for a major surprise," and I am surprised. I'm surprised that my tendency to blame people is that strong and that devastating.

I'm trying to better understand my current tendency to blame. As I already concluded, at the base of our tendency to blame others is the common way in which we deal with conflicts; we seek compromises. Compromise is the attempt to share a finite cake. When do we find an acceptable compromise? When the perception is that the cake is not very important, or that it's not too small to start with. But when the cake seems too small, seeking a compromise is a situation in which the more you win, the more I lose; seeking a compromise is, by definition, a win-lose approach. As human beings we always have our own win in mind; we are "programmed" for self-interest. Therefore, when we are involved in a conflict, in a situation that is handled as a win-lose situation, we will be more protective than generous. And when we are not satisfied with the end result we'll naturally blame the one that pushed us into that unsatisfactory situation; we'll blame the other side. No wonder that as a result of our life experience we develop the tendency to blame the other party whenever we encounter a conflict situation.

Instead we should adopt the belief in Inherent Simplicity. Our approach to conflicts should be based on trying to remove an underlying assumption so that the conflict will vanish. Removing the conflict paves the way to find the desired change. We'll then be focused on expanding the existing cake rather than fighting over our share of a finite, too-limited cake. It's what we call seeking a win-win solution. What Father is actually claiming by "Harmony exists in any relationship between people" is that a win-win solution always exists. Good. I feel much more comfortable with this terminology.

This sheds a new light on Father's insistence that one should accept that harmony always exists—that our starting point should be that for any relationship there is a change that will bring the parties to each achieve what they need from the relationship. It doesn't matter if it actually does exist, what matters is that one should approach a strained relationship with the determination that it does, rather than finding refuge in blaming the other party. If we allow ourselves to reach the stage where we blame the other party, our emotions will start to blind us. What is then the chance that we'll devote the time and concentration needed to seriously look for the change that will foster harmony? Nil. This means that in situations that do not have an acceptable compromise, we have nothing to lose and we have so much to gain if we adopt Father's advice.

Father's approach is not philosophical; it is pragmatic! I feel much better.

Searching for a win-win solution requires that we find the assumption that can be removed, but this is sometimes quite difficult. Maybe my new understanding provides a shortcut?

Reaching a win-win solution enlarges the cake. The bigger the cake, the greater the chance we'll get a bigger piece. So, if we want to get a bigger piece, the prudent way to deal with a conflict is to make sure that all efforts are concentrated on finding a win-win solution. Bearing in mind that subconsciously we always try to protect our own win, isn't it prudent to consciously start constructing the win-win solution by seeking the other party's win? Won't that increase the chance of finding such a solution?

Unfortunately, that will not work. For example, taking the contractor's case, to start with the win for the other side (the brand company) will be to yield to accepting lower prices from the brands, which is exactly the opposite of what the contractor wants. Looking for the other side's win does not remove the conflict, rather it leads directly into the grip of the conflict—leads directly to a lose situation.

I'm disappointed. I had expected that following logically the superiority of win-win solutions would lead me to a correct starting point, but apparently it doesn't. Something is wrong. I take a deep breath and read Father's report again, trying to see what he was doing.

As I speculated, Father does start constructing a win-win solution by seeking the other party's win. But not the win that is in conflict. He is looking for a different, but not less important win. For example, as the starting point for his first attempt he uses the fact that the brands want the contractors to hold their inventory for them. "What the brands love, almost to the extent that they like to further reduce the price they pay to the contractor, is that the contractor will hold the inventory for them."

And when he realizes that he needs a solution that will enable getting higher prices from the brands he looks for something that the brands want even more than a reduction in price. And he finds such a win for the brands: much higher inventory turns. "As a matter of fact, knowing that all brands are currently struggling to find ways to increase their inventory turns, I think that they will be interested in such an offer to the extent that the contractor can use it effectively to increase its margins."

If we want our win to be bigger we have to ensure that the other side's win will be bigger. Is it always possible to find a win for the other side that is bigger than what the other side is explicitly going after?

If there is a bigger win for the other party, why doesn't the other party ask for it? If it is so important, how come they don't demand it?

And then it dawns on me. We have discussed it already. We said that people, and companies, lower expectations when they use protective mechanisms to camouflage from themselves the big chronic problems; the problems that they already gave up on resolving. If a party is using such protective mechanisms (and who isn't?) it means that it is numb to its biggest needs; it will not explicitly ask for what it really needs because it doesn't believe that there is a way to get it.

Now I understand why Father said that those who are not prepared will be blind to the stream of opportunities life presents them. We are not in the shoes of the other party; we are not suffering from his protective mechanisms. If we just try to really understand the other side, we are in a better position then he is to recognize how to fulfill his major needs. Nobody, not even Father, said that you can have a harmonious relationship with people you don't care about—if you don't care to invest the time and effort to know them and their true needs.

Amazing how it all ties together: the claim that harmony exists in any relationship between people; the concept of win-win; the recommendation to start with looking for a different big (or bigger) win for the other party; and the ability to identify the bigger wins through the camouflaged problems. All these concepts are now complementing each other; they are all parts of the same picture.

Harmony: "the quality of forming a pleasing and consistent whole." I think that I now understand what Father meant when he talked about scientists commenting with awe on that harmony.

It feels good. It feels right.

What is needed now is to sharpen my abilities to think clearly. I turn back to finish reading his report. Will my new understanding help me to follow it more easily?

CHAPTER 10

Never Say "I Know"
(Continued)

How can they get higher margins? I couldn't think of an additional way to get a higher price from the company's clients, the brand companies. So what about bypassing them and selling directly to retail?

Usually this avenue is not feasible for a contractor since it actually demands building a new type of company. It is one thing to have the ability to cut and sew fabric into garments according to given designs; it is a totally different ability to design new collections of garments and to do it three times a year in pace with the changing fashion. But in this particular case our company already has this ability. It does have its own collections, and in its country these collections compete well with the big brands' collections. As a matter of fact, in their country they are number three in selling their own sports apparel, ahead of much bigger and better-known brands. So, it seems that if we want to increase the company's margin, we just have to concentrate more on sales directly to the shops. And since they have almost saturated their small country—they have their shops in every major location—they will have to approach shops outside of their country. Considering the markup of brands, this will not just increase the company's margins, it will explode them.

Isn't it obvious? Well, from harsh experience, I've learned to be very careful answering this question. On the one hand, I do recognize that all good solutions have one thing in common—they are obvious, but only in hindsight. Always, once I finally verbalize a good solution to a major problem, I'm disappointed with myself for wasting so much time before I reached the obvious.

But, on the other hand, I also learned not to just admire, but actually to respect, peoples' experience and intuition. If the solution is correct, if the solution is really so obvious, how come people haven't used this solution a long time ago? It must be that something, an erroneous assumption that they took for granted as an indisputable fact of life, caused them to dismiss this solution; blocked them from even trying to implement it. So until I clearly recognize and verify such a blocking assumption I don't know if my new solution is obvious, or just stupid.

Why hadn't this company tried to sell directly to shops outside their own country? It must be because it has the name recognition, the brand name, mainly within the borders of their country. In other words, outside its country it is a nonbrand company. And the managers of the company had learned that to build a brand name takes time, a lot of time. And money, a lot of money. The bigger the country, the bigger the sums of money required. It is obvious that to build a brand name in a sizable country is beyond their current financial and managerial abilities.

But why is having a brand name so important? Why are they convinced that as long as the company hasn't yet established a real brand name in the territory in which a shop is located it will not be economical to try and persuade the shops to carry their collections?

It is, probably, because shops know that merchandise that carries a known name will sell, and they are reluctant to take the risk of buying nonbrand merchandise, merchandise that might not sell well enough. The shops' reluctance is logical because the constraint of most shops is display space (and cash). Carrying merchandise that might not sell well is actually wasting the constraint (the opposite of exploit), and therefore reduces the overall sales of the shop.

We can proceed from here in two ways. One is systematic, logical and meticulous. The other is bold, daring and not less logical. There are actually many more ways to proceed, but since they are not logical I'll ignore them.

Do you know Robert Frost's poem, *The Road Not Taken*?

> Two roads diverged in a yellow wood,
> And sorry I could not travel both
> And be one traveler, long I stood
> And looked down one as far as I could
> To where it bent in the undergrowth;

First, let's look down the meticulous road as far as we can. It is meticulous and also boring, so please don't fall asleep before we start to travel the other, much more exciting, road.

Shops might be reluctant to carry nonbrand products, but it is a fact that many shops do carry a lot of nonbrand products. So, it must be that the managers of our company know that it is possible to sell to shops outside their country, but they don't really try to do it because they are convinced that it might lead to losses rather than profits. Let's carefully examine this conviction because the alternative is simply to give up on the idea of selling directly to the shops.

First, let's get rid of the more banal way. If the shops are reluctant to buy nonbrand merchandise because it is too risky, the company should reduce the shops' risk by offering the goods on consignment. This is a lousy suggestion. Offering the goods on consignment is very risky for the supplier, since there is a high chance that most of the merchandise will be shipped back at the end of the season. And it is bad for the shop because, consignment or not, blocking a shelf with merchandise that doesn't move well reduces the sales of the shop.

The shops that do carry nonbrand merchandise are aware of the risk of holding too much slow-moving merchandise. They reduce the risk through lowering the price of those goods to the end consumer; they increase the chance of sales of the nonbrand products by fixing the end price of nonbrand products to be substantially lower than the brands' prices. But, at the same time, the shops are also making sure that their margins will be adequate, which means they will pay much lower prices to the nonbrand providers. How low can our company go and still make nice profits?

Let's assume that the shops will sell the company's garments for a price that is half the price of the brand garment. That means that if the shop maintains the same markup regardless of whether or not the garment is a brand garment, the shops will pay our company half the price the shops pay for an equivalent brand garment. Half the price the brands get is still much more than what the brands are currently paying to the contractor. That means that it behooves the company to sell directly to retail since, in doing so, the company will make gross margins that are several times bigger than the current gross margins it sees selling to the brands.

Let's not be hasty to jump to such a conclusion. Remember, the managers of a company do have a lot of experience and intuition. Therefore, we can assume that they are oblivious to the obvious only in cases where we clearly pinpointed an erroneous assumption that blocked them from seeing the obvious. In our case, did we identify such a blocking erroneous assumption?

No!

So it must be that something is wrong; that I've ignored something essential in doing the above calculation.

The expected margins are based on the assumption that the likely sales price to the shops will *not* be less than half the price the shops pay for an equivalent brand garment. Is this crucial assumption solid?

As we said, when the company tries to sell in other countries it is a nonbrand company; it does not have any real competitive edge. Are there other nonbrand companies that sell in those countries? Many. Many nonbrands, none having a competitive edge, are the ideal conditions for the buyers of the shops to try to squeeze down the purchase price. And they are experts in squeezing. Under the reality of a price war, can we safely assume that the selling price to the shops will be as high as half the brand price? Let's ask it in a different way. Are the existing nonbrand companies making a fortune? Not at all. Some make a living, some struggle, some are going out of business, but rarely do we hear about nonbrand companies in apparel making a fortune unless they succeeded to build something specific that gives them a competitive edge in a niche market. A price of half the brands' price seems a little too optimistic.

What is behind the "bent in the undergrowth"? The tendency is still to do some checks, including checking the price the shops are paying for nonbrand garments and checking the cost of putting in a sales force to sell to shops. It will take time, effort and some investment, but there is a chance that as a result of extensive checks, the conclusion will be that it is a viable road. Maybe.

Now let's follow the *other* road, the bold, daring road.

As we said, the main reason that shops are reluctant to buy from a nonbrand company is that the risk that the merchandise will not sell well enough is much higher for nonbrand merchandise. We can be totally relaxed if we find a way to reduce that risk to a level that is even below the risk that shops take when they buy brand garments. Daring? You bet, but the real question is: Is it possible?

To answer this question we have to first assess the risk

the shops are taking when they carry a brand garment.

Is there any risk for the shop when it buys a brand garment? We know that there is a major risk. We know that even when the shop buys brand garments there are a lot of relatively slow movers. Some (about thirty percent) are so slow that a shop has to carry them for a few months and then it is only able to sell them (at a loss) at the end-of-the-season clearance sales.

Allowing the shops to buy based on actual consumption rather than forecast, plus offering the return of slow movers for a full refund (and the mechanism of "return this, take that instead") the company reduces the shops' risk to a bare minimum, while improving substantially the exploitation of the shops' shelf space. Let's do some calculations to realize the financial impact of such a unique service on the shop's profitability.

Let's conservatively estimate the total increase in sales (due to fewer shortages, and a much higher percentage of high runners) to be just fifty percent. For the shop this is an increase in sales that is not associated with any increase in overhead or employee costs. What is the resulting impact on the shop's profitability? Even though most shops mark up the price by a hundred percent, the vast majority of the shops do not make more than five percent net profit on sales. For such shops, a fifty percent increase in sales means that their profit on our company's products will increase by at least a factor of five, versus comparable goods purchased from a conventional manufacturer.

It stands to reason that when a sale to the shop is done in the proper way—explaining the logic that clearly shows the benefits to the shops rather than talking mainly about the garments themselves—most shops that are not dedicated to specific brands will accept the company's offer. A shop will probably start with a test collection, but within weeks that test will expand, creating a happy and loyal outlet.

What about our company's investment? With such a mafia offer, the company should choose to concentrate its sales efforts on a densely populated area that can be served by one regional warehouse. The amount of sales (potential sales are larger than several times what our company's capacity can supply) and profits will easily dwarf the relatively small investment in inventory.

All in all, it looks like this approach is an obvious winner. But we are not the first ones to look for a solution for selling nonbrand products directly to shops. Many, who are not less bright or less meticulous than we, have tried to solve it. How come we have succeeded where they all failed?

They tried to find a way to reduce the gap between the risks the shop is taking buying from a nonbrand as compared with the risks of buying from a brand. We have approached it differently. We increased the challenge to the level of impossibility—instead of trying to reduce the gap, we dared to think about reversing the gap.

Two roads diverged in a wood, and I–
I took the one less traveled by,
And that has made all the difference.

CHAPTER 11

How Many Opportunities Are There?

This time it was easier to follow Father's logic. To start with, I knew where he was headed. As expected, he started by exploring for a big win for the other side— the shops—a win that is more than just buying at lower prices. That was the key; identifying the win and then finding the way to satisfy it.

For this company, selling directly to the shops is now a viable addition to selling to the brand companies. Are there more alternatives? There must be, because he started this report by stating that his renewed analysis yielded not one, but three, additions to the body of knowledge. His report details two new solutions. Where is the third one?

I bet he planted this comment so that when one of his people comes to him with this observation, he will have the ideal platform to teach them how to derive the additional solution. Knowing my father, he would play such a trick only if he had already paved the way for finding the third solution by the process he used in constructing the second solution.

Can I do it? Where would I start to look for the third solution? I start to realize the answer when I force myself to stop. I don't want to become a strategy expert. I should concentrate on squeezing from Father the answer to a much more important question. How does one learn to think clearly so that they will be better able to live a full life? Have I distilled everything I could from the report?

My eyes are stuck on the title, "Never say 'I know.'" That doesn't make too much sense. Suppose one has implemented a good solution and it did work, substantially improving the situation. I think that such a person is rightfully entitled to proudly announce, "I know!"

Father is careful with words. He would not use a strong word like "never" if he didn't mean it.

"Never say I know." Why does he claim this? Is it because he thinks that the conviction that we know will block us from further improving the situation?

This can't be. This conviction, that one knows, is not likely to block anybody from seeing that the situation can be further improved. Everyone knows that there is always room for improvement. I keep thinking. He would not give such a warning in the title of a report unless it was really important.

Improvement. If we keep improving a system we will reach the stage that the system is quite good. We can still improve it but we can no longer expect to gain as much as we did at the beginning; the reality of diminishing returns kicks in. But whenever Father gives an example of an improvement it is always a major breakthrough, a fundamental new insight that propels the entire subject to a new level.

Have I stumbled on the fourth obstacle? Does the impression that "we know" block us from using our intuition and brainpower? It certainly looks like it. A person who is convinced that the system is functioning well, that whatever there is to know about the system is known by them, that what is left is just to continue polishing, will never bother to spend the time and effort looking for a breakthrough. Did he warn us never to say "I know" because he thinks that we should never be satisfied with diminishing returns? That the next breakthrough is always waiting around the corner?

I think I'm getting ahead of myself. Rather than occupying my mind with how to improve a situation that is already good, shouldn't I concentrate on how to be more proficient at improving the more common situations, those that are not yet good; to concentrate now on learning how to systematically overcome the first three obstacles; to learn how to generate meaningful opportunities and then how to turn enough of them into successes?

It might be the more prudent thing to do but I can't restrain my thoughts. I continue to wonder if there is always a way to jump a situation to a new level, no matter how good it is to start with. If there is, it has far-reaching ramifications. I always thought that the best opportunities are opened when we overcome a blockage, when we realize how to improve a bad situation. But if everything, including situations that are already good, can be substantially improved, doesn't it imply that there are opportunities all around us?

In order to live a full life, one needs suitable opportunities. Enough of them. Until a minute ago I was convinced that suitable opportunities are rare. But if my interpretation of "Never say 'I know'" is correct, that any situation can be substantially improved, then Father actually claims that there are abundant opportunities; they are everywhere we look. That is too good to be true.

I am building a castle on quicksand; on my interpretation of a single word. Before I proceed I must verify with Father if my interpretation is correct. Hopefully it means receiving another one of his reports.

CHAPTER 12

Short Shelf Life Products*

When an industry is already operating in line with a TOC solution, do we still have anything of significance to offer?

Last week I made an audit visit to a relatively large company that manufactures flour and maize. This company sells these ingredients in bulk to other manufacturers, in packages of half a kilo to 2.5 kilos to retailers, and its highest-margin product is bread, produced in eight large bakeries and representing about thirty percent of the total sales. Increasing sales of a significant, high-margin product has much more of an impact than increasing sales of a low-margin product. No wonder that when I first met them, two years ago, my inclination was to focus on the bread.

Since bread is a consumer goods product, the relevant TOC solution is the Distribution Solution, which is based on increasing the frequency of orders and/or deliveries.

---

*This report was written and circulated to the Goldratt Group in March 2007. For the purpose of this book it was slightly modified to enable easy reading for readers who are not familiar with the operations of the Goldratt Group.

We are used to environments where frequencies of once a week or even once a month are common. From our experience in regular products, we have learned that a delivery frequency of once a day is enough to ensure no shortages; increasing the frequency to higher than once a day does not increase availability and/or sales. But bread is already delivered to each shop every morning. Considering the current high frequency of bread delivery, do we still have anything of significance to offer? Before we give up and restrict our attention to the company's other products, the lower margin products that have conventional frequency of orders and/or deliveries, maybe we should continue to ask: Why is bread delivered once a day?

It is because bread has a short shelf life.

What typifies a short shelf life product is that freshness is a major issue. From my days in the army, I remember that when we asked the cook, "Can we have fresh bread?" he would reply, "You want bread that was baked today? Come back tomorrow."

Yes, there is a big difference if the bread was baked today or yesterday. There is also a difference between warm bread that was baked half an hour ago and a loaf of bread that was baked two hours ago. But, is there a difference between loaves baked two hours ago or eight hours ago? Not really. Therefore, it looks like unless the company finds a way to offer bread directly from the oven, from the point of view of the consumer, delivery once a day is the right frequency.

Before we conclude that delivery once a day is optimal for our company, let's review the impact a short shelf life product has on the retailer. Suppose that whatever is not sold today cannot be sold tomorrow: surpluses turn into obsolescence. Or, suppose the less extreme scenario, that whatever is not sold today has a lesser chance of being sold tomorrow, and keeping it on the shelves for an extra day causes a bad impression on the consumers.

The bread produced by this company is sliced and wrapped in plastic; the product life is estimated to be four days. The expiration date is, by law, printed prominently on the plastic bag. Since the shelf life is more than a day and since customers are sensitive to expiration dates, the second, less extreme scenario is applicable to this company's situation.

Even though the retailer wants to have the product available, he must consider the impact that leftovers (products older than one day) have on the business. One can expect that when the daily demand is not precisely known, the retailer will tend to be on the conservative side and as a result, towards the end of the day, the product might not always be available in the shop. Therefore, moving from once a day to a higher frequency of delivery may result in an increase in sales.

How big of an increase?

Well, it is a function of the level of conservatism of the retailer. Being aware that one cannot be sure to enter a shop towards the end of the day and find a decent looking loaf of bread, I estimated that increasing the delivery to twice per day might result in a not negligible increase in sales. Since I did expect shortages to be mainly in the afternoon and since most of the demand is in the morning, my highest hopes did not exceed a thirty percent increase, and I was not going to be overly surprised if the increase would be less than ten percent.

But this change in frequency of delivery also has an effect on cost. The gross margin of these products is around forty to fifty percent of sales, and distribution costs are only a few (three to five) percent of sales. Therefore, as long as the increase in sales will be more than ten percent, even if the company has to double its distribution costs, it will still positively impact its net profit.*

As for production, splitting the demand to two times a day has mainly positive effects. So it all depends on how much sales will increase due to changing the mode of operation to two deliveries a day. If it is more than ten percent, it is good. If it is close to thirty percent, it is very good.

If you run the numbers you should wonder why I claim that an increase in sales of close to thirty percent is very good. When there is an increase of thirty percent on a product line that is only thirty percent of the business and when the materials cost is half of the selling price, you will see an increase in profit of only five percent of sales (.3 x .3 x .5 = 5%). This number is so far from what is needed to reach a quantum jump in performance that I should regard it as just a distraction.

---

*Bread is unique in the sense that the shops mandate that it must be available in the morning. As a result, the bakeries for the company are strategically located all over this large country, and all shipments are done within the span of a few hours. Most of the day, the transportation fleet is standing idle. It is likely that a second delivery a day will not require any increase to the fleet.

A thirty percent increase is very good because the key sentence in the above analysis is, "One can expect that when the daily demand is not precisely known, the retailer will tend to be on the conservative side." To realize that this sentence might hold the key for a quantum leap in performance one should examine the prime reasons for uncertainties in the daily demand.

When a particular type of bread is selling fifty loaves a day, one can expect that in a particular day sales might be sixty loaves or forty loaves but, except for rare days, one will not expect sales of only twenty loaves. In other words, the reasonable variability in the daily demand for such a product is around twenty percent. But if we examine a product that is selling on average only five units per day, the reasonable expectation is that it might sell only one or two in a particular day. In other words, the variability is much higher. The smaller the number of items sold per day, the higher the uncertainty in the forecast of the quantity that will be sold on any given day. Therefore, we should expect that the retailer will be much more conservative when ordering the low-running items. Also, it stands to reason that the less experience the retailer has with the product the higher his conservatism will be.

How does the above relate to our company's situation?

Bread is one of the few products that we do have a lot of experience with. We all know that there is a huge difference in price between common bread and the more fancy breads, like croissants or raisin bread. We also know that even though the price of fancy bread might be three or four times higher than the price of a common bread, the ingredients are unlikely to be more than twice as expensive. The throughput of the more fancy breads dwarfs the throughput of the common bread. Using these estimates, if the throughput of common bread is fifty percent of the selling price and is equal to two units of money, the throughput of fancy bread is likely to be eight units of money. But the number of items sold of each of the fancy breads is much smaller than the number of items sold of the common bread. Moreover, when the company offers new fancy bread to the shop, by definition the retailer has less experience with that product. Therefore, it must be that the conservatism of the retailer is severely dampening both the availability of fancy breads on its shelves and the introduction of new types.

If a second delivery in a day will result in an increase in sales as high as thirty percent, it means that the fact that the company delivers twice a day is a very effective way to deal with the conservatism of the retailer. It means that the doors for a huge increase in sales of the more fancy breads will be wide open. Considering the hefty throughput of those breads the company will be able to further reduce the conservatism of the retailer by offering to take back, for full refund, the leftovers. One more fancy loaf sold compensates for two loaves taken back.

Let's reasonably speculate on the potential impact by following the logical chain we have already constructed. If the increase in sales for the common bread will be thirty percent then we must conclude that the second delivery effectively removes the conservatism of the retailer. Since for the fancy breads the number of loaves sold per day is much smaller than the corresponding number for common bread, the current impact of the retailer's conservatism on the sales of fancy bread is much higher than for the common bread. Therefore, removing the conservatism factor will cause a much larger increase in sales for the fancy bread. We are talking about a sales increase of the fancy breads that is probably twice as high as the increase for the common bread. Add to it the new ease of introducing a whole spectrum of new fancy breads, and the resulting increase is anybody's guess. Now multiply this increase with the spectacularly better throughput of fancy bread. We are no longer talking about an increase in profit equal to five percent of current sales, but much higher percentages.

What was left to do was to check; to run an experiment with shops representing the different market segments, from supermarkets in big towns to mom-and-pop shops in rural areas. But since at that stage the expected increase in profit from bread was based on a speculation, I did not neglect to deal also with the packaged mill products.

Here we are standing on more solid ground. We know that our distribution solution, moving from the current frequency of delivering once a week (and to many stores even once a month) to a frequency of once a day, will certainly increase sales while substantially reducing the inventory levels the retail shop is holding. This provides solid ground upon which to build new relationships with the retailers; relationships that will enable expansion to many more stores. Increasing the company's sales per shop while also increasing the number of shops is probably enough to reach the Viable Vision (the desired quantum leap in performance).

Of course, since the existing infrastructure is based on

supply to retailer orders, the switch to supply to actual sales to consumers requires major changes in many functions. Production is traditionally used to the mode of operation of produce-to-order, while augmenting the retailer orders with internal stock orders. This mentality, of striving for full activation of the mills' capacity, must be replaced with the much more demanding mode of operation of produce-to-availability.

Distribution has to go through as big a change: the change from push-pull mode, to the replenishment to actual consumption mode; replenishment—rather than pull—from the mills, and replenishment—rather than push—to the stores. Not less important, distribution must put the proper systems in place to ensure that the target level of each SKU is constantly monitored.

The biggest change is, of course, in sales. It is not a triviality to switch from constantly pushing each store to buy more, especially toward the end of the month and more so toward the end of the quarter, into establishing "partnerships" according to the real needs of the store; striving to increase the return on inventory of the store by agreeing on the right inventory levels and then simply replenishing the actual consumption.

In the little over a year since the project started, all the groundwork has been successfully implemented. The bakeries' flexibility improved to the extent that the cycle to produce all types of bread has been reduced from twenty-four hours to about eight hours while increasing the volume baked (that means that the lead time, from the first loaf exiting the oven until the truck, loaded with all the bread variety needed to service the stores, leaves the shipping dock, has been reduced from almost twenty-four hours to about eight hours). This puts the bakeries at an excellent starting point to dramatically expand the number of different types of bread they can provide.

The mills demonstrated that the switch to producing to availability is not only possible, it was achieved while increasing the mills' effective capacity. The computerized production systems, both in the bakeries and the mills, are not just functioning well, they are fully embraced by the production personnel, which is no trivial achievement.

All the distribution warehouses are replenished well; the system is humming. Inventory has been reduced, coupled with a substantial reduction in the number of shortages. A small paragraph that describes a big accomplishment.

But most importantly, the test of the impact of more frequent deliveries on sales has been launched. The results of the test, conducted in fourteen representative shops, have been monitored for the last four months.

As expected, for the mill products (the small packages of flour and maize sold through retail), the sales to the shops went down initially since the excess inventories had to be flushed out. As was also expected, sales then started to pick up nicely and stabilized at a level that is significantly above the starting level of sales. What was less expected was that sales stabilized at a level that is ninety percent higher than the sales in the corresponding months of last year. This high level of sales was sustained for the last three months. Let me explain why this high increase is something of a surprise.

The replenishment solution impacts sales through two different channels. One channel is the direct channel. Proper replenishment almost eliminates shortages and fewer shortages translates directly to more sales. The second channel of impact, which we have come to realize is as big as the first, is due to the fact that proper replenishment reduces the inventories of slow movers dramatically. As a result, sales increase due to the fact that having fewer slow movers frees up more of the shelf space and also frees up the attention of the sales personnel for the faster movers.

The bigger the number of SKUs a shop is holding the bigger are the two effects. Since there are only thirty SKUs of mill products offered and a shop is holding, on average, fewer than fifteen SKUs, this impressive ninety percent increase is more than I expected, but it is still within the spread we see in other environments that have switched to the replenishment solution.

A demonstrated ninety percent increase in sales is ensuring that the replenishment offer will be very attractive to any shop and that distribution cost considerations (being so small relative to the additional throughput) will not stand in the way of a major expansion. If the same level of increased sales will be maintained when this better service is done on a grand scale—and I cannot see any real reason why it should not hold—the Viable Vision target can be achieved much before the target date, which is still two-and-a-half years in the future.

What about the bread? What are the results of this field test for the impact of increasing the bread delivery to twice a day?

My real delight and astonishment comes from the results recorded at the same shops for the bread. From day one, bread sales increased by over a hundred percent! The exact average for all fourteen shops for the four-month test is 118%.

Delight and astonishment. Let me first expand on the "delight" part.

Such an enormous increase clearly indicates that the second delivery a day had wiped out the retailer conservatism. The door is wide open for the really hefty-margin products: the fancy breads. If the numbers reported in the test are real it is clear that in the remaining two-and-a-half years it will be a walk in the park to surpass the once ambitious target. But we better restrain the desire to immediately spread to all the many thousands of shops before we know more precisely the causes and effects governing the sales increase. Now is the time to expand the test to about a hundred shops; to introduce a variety of the fancy breads and to monitor which parameters impact the sales and throughput increases.

Why am I "astonished" by an increase of a hundred percent in bread sales, especially in light of the fact that I've already seen such (and higher) numbers in regular products (textiles, for example)?

Go over the explanation provided for my expectation that the maximum increase will be thirty percent. Do you find any logical mistake in that prediction? The prediction was for maximum thirty percent increase. Where did this increase in sales of over one hundred percent come from?

In all previous cases, when the better replenishment led to an increase in sales, I assumed that the increase was at the expense of a reduction in sales of the competitors. But in the bread case, such an explanation cannot possibly be correct. Our company is big; it provides about thirty percent of the bread sold in the country. It is not present in all shops, so it must be that in the shops it is present in, it represents about fifty percent of the bread sold by these shops. If the increase in sales was mainly at the expense of the competitors, it would mean that the competitors were, for all practical purposes, wiped out from those shops. But that did not happen, so it must be that the increase in sales came from another avenue.

In the morning our company does not have a real advantage over its competitors, but that is not the case in the afternoon. Maybe the much better availability in the afternoon attracted customers of other shops? If that would be the case we should witness a drop in the company sales in other nearby shops, shops that were still serviced only once a day. But that did not happen either, not in any significant amount.

So the only explanation I can come up with is that the customers of the test shops are buying more bread; they probably have doubled their bread purchases.

At first I found it difficult to accept such an explanation, but after examining my own family's behavior it started to become more plausible. At least in my home, when anyone in my family has a choice between old bread and a newly purchased loaf, almost always the choice will be to eat the new loaf, even if it means that the old one will eventually end up in the garbage can. Couple it with the fact that more and more people do their grocery shopping after working hours, and it is no longer surprising that good availability of fresh bread in the afternoon can lead to such a major increase in purchases of bread.

Actually, after discussing it with several people I started to wonder why it had been so hard for me to accept that the increase in sales in the test shops comes mainly from an actual increase in purchases—from an actual increase in demand.

Is it because I accept what I learned in economics as a given? Accept it without trying to check if it meets my life experience?

In economics I've learned that there is supply and demand, that prices are the result of the level of supply compared with the level of demand. I've learned (maybe the problem is in me and not in my teachers) that supply and demand are independent variables; that if a company increases its sales, it is at the expense of the sales of its competitors. That the cake is finite. That it is a zero-sum game.

This certainly has an effect on how we currently analyze a company's potential. When a company already has a sixty percent market share, we assume that once the company succeeds in building a decisive competitive edge the maximum increase in sales will be the remainder of the existing market, the other forty percent. We always assumed that if the company wants a bigger increase the company will have to expand to new markets or provide new products in the same markets. Can it be that we should think differently, that we should at least entertain the possibility that the offer that *does* give the company a decisive competitive edge simultaneously also increases the existing market? At least as far as consumer goods are concerned? Can I accept that better supply (of the same product and while maintaining or even increasing the price) is increasing, substantially, the demand? That supply and demand are variables that are strongly dependent? Hmm...

CHAPTER 13

The Sky is
Not the Limit

I'm driving Father home from the airport.

"Have you read the report I sent you few days ago?" he asks.

I was waiting for this question. "Before you ask me what I deduce from it," I say, "let me ask you something. From the report it's apparent that you were surprised by the increase in sales, both in the packaged products and the bread; it was much higher than the increase you expected."

"Yes, it was. So what's your question?"

"You taught me that the most precious opportunities to deepen our knowledge are whenever reality is significantly different than our expectation. Most people will just accept results that are better than expectations with delight and move on. But I suspect that you didn't just rush forward; I expect that you took the time to investigate the reasons for the discrepancy. If so, did you find anything significant?"

Apparently pleased, he gently strokes my hand. "Not only did I ask for more details, I felt so uncomfortable with the numbers that I asked the president and COO of that company to look further into how the test was done and then join me in my office in Holland for three days. They are exceptionally bright and practical people, so I knew that no matter what, we were bound to have a good time. And yes, we made significant progress in those three days."

I'm pleased with myself. When I first finished reading his report I was quite disappointed. Here I am asking Father to answer a very important question: Can any situation, no matter how good it is to start with, be substantially improved? And as an answer I get a report that shows how one specific situation was improved. Should I deduce from this that if one situation can be improved, any other situation can?

Moreover, I don't accept that the situation that was described in the report was very good to start with; the fact that replenishing daily is the tradition in bread doesn't yet imply that the situation was already very good.

No wonder that my initial impression was that Father didn't answer my question. I even suspected that he didn't make a serious attempt to understand my question. Frankly, I felt somewhat offended.

Good thing he had been abroad, so I couldn't rush to his house and confront him. It gave me time to tame my tendency to blame, and instead examine other possibilities that might explain why I received this report as an answer to my question. After raising and dismissing some other possibilities I noticed that he had stressed that the results of the test were not in line with his expectations. So maybe Father sent me this report not as an answer but as an introduction to the answer; maybe the real eye-opening case is to follow. That was a more plausible, and less aggravating, possibility. Now it looks like my speculation is on the nose.

"I'm sure that you had a good time in Holland with

those guys," I say cheerfully. "Are you going to tell me what progress you made or do I have to beg for it?"

"Just keep your eyes on the road," he laughs. "It was no surprise that the percentages reported for the increase in sales were wrong. It turned out that four out of the fourteen shops that composed the test were new clients—shops that the company was not doing business with before. You see, at the outset we predicted that the more frequent replenishment would be attractive to the extent that it would help to convince more shops to carry the company's products. This is important to them, so naturally they checked it as well. The problem was that when they compiled the numbers, they took the total amount they sold to all these fourteen shops and compared it to the amount sold a year ago. Of course when you include shops that a year ago you sold nothing to and you report the results in term of a percentage increase, you get a big distortion."

"But that's easy to correct," I say. "What was the real increase?"

"The actual increase per shop was around sixty percent. That is in line with what we expected for the packaged products. As for the bread, it just highlighted that the conservatism of the shop owners—their tendency to make sure that they will not end up with old loaves—is higher then what I assumed originally."

I start to become a little itchy. That's it? That's the whole story? Can't be. "How much time did it take you to realize that the new numbers don't change the picture? Fifteen minutes? What did you do in the remaining three days?"

"Obviously we rethought the solution." He grins.

"Why?" I ask. "Everything now fits, and the results are better then you needed to ensure a quantum leap in the company's performance. What caused you to rethink the solution?" I slow the car down. Once we reach home I won't stand a chance competing against his grandchildren for his attention.

"You are right that the results are more than satisfactory, but darling, not everything fits."

Responding to my surprised expression he elaborates. "When I first did the analysis I noticed that the company assumed that the orders the shops were giving were the best prediction for the next day's demand. That is the assumption that I elected to challenge. I speculated that the demand is higher than the orders because the orders are influenced by the conservatism of the shop owner. As you read, I'd had no idea of the magnitude of the conservatism, but now we are standing on much more solid ground. We know that the conservatism is playing a major role. We know that it is bigger than what I allowed myself to hope for. The resulting increase is not ten percent or even thirty percent, it is sixty percent. Don't these results also highlight that I didn't fully understand the *reasons* for that conservatism?"

So that is how he gets the drive to go after better and better solutions. He is careful not to think that he knows, careful to the extent that he is alert to every sign that indicates that he doesn't know. That reminds me of the conclusion I reached earlier: thinking like a true scientist means being 'humbly arrogant.' Humble to have the conviction that you don't know; arrogant to have the conviction that you can develop the knowledge.

"As you said, Father, the most precious opportunities to deepen our knowledge appear when reality is significantly different than our expectations. So how did you go about developing the better understanding of the shops' conservatism? Please try to be as detailed as you can."

"I'll try. How does one dive into the reasons for the

shop's conservatism? The conservatism must be a function of the damage that the shop will suffer from being stuck with an old loaf in comparison to the benefit the shop gains from selling one more loaf. At the outset I knew that since the company is also the flour provider their margins on bread are relatively large; close to fifty percent. It's composed of the margin of their wheat mill and the margin of their bakery. But I didn't bother to check the margin of a shop, I just assumed that it is the regular supermarket margin, around thirty to thirty-five percent. What I learned in our meeting in Holland was that since bread is a basic product, so basic that the shop has to provide it, the shop's margin is very low, about fifteen percent of the selling price."

"But that means," I say, quite surprised, "that one unsold loaf erases the profit of five sold loaves. No wonder that the conservatism of the shop is high."

"So high that we were asking ourselves if delivering two times a day is just reducing, rather than eliminating, this conservatism. What do you think?"

"If I'm the shop owner," I answer, "I would make sure that I'm not stuck with old bread. Since the demand fluctuates from day to day, even when there are two deliveries a day I will still order less than the expected average demand."

He releases a long puff of pipe smoke through the open window. "That was our conclusion also. So the next obvious questions were: How can we make sure that we erased, totally, the conservatism of the shop so that the amount we sell to the shop is equal to the real demand; and how can we verify that we accomplished it?"

"Please wait." I signal with my hand.

The hardest thing to do is to struggle to find an answer to a problem when we believe that there is a high chance that it doesn't have an answer; it is so easy to give up. That is why Father recommends starting with the conviction that a better solution exists for sure. In the case we are discussing now I am in that frame of mind; I am convinced that there is a solution because I know that Father found one. Is this conviction by itself enough to find the solution? I don't think so, but this is an excellent opportunity to test it.

"Let me try to figure it out myself," I say without much conviction. "What can be done to erase the conservatism of the shop?"

I don't have a clue. But I'm in no position to declare defeat. How does he even think about such a question?

He thinks cause and effect; if we want to eliminate the effect we should eliminate the cause. If we want to erase the conservatism of the shop we should erase the cause for it. What did we say is the cause for the conservatism? It is the disproportional negative effect of a loaf that the shop is stuck with. What can be done to reduce the damage? That's not enough. What can be done to eliminate it? What can the company do to ensure that the shop will not suffer at all from having a loaf that became old?

The company can take it back, for a full refund. But that will just shift the damage to the company. Yes, but the company can more easily absorb it; the company's margin per loaf is much higher. Will it still be a good proposition for the company? Will the increase in sales compensate for the cost of obsolescence? I'm not sure.

Hesitantly I say, "Should the company take back yesterday's bread for a full refund?"

"That is exactly what we contemplated as well," he replies. "Of course, I wasted some time struggling with the numbers to see if it pays off before I noticed that they were not at all bothered by it. When I asked why they accepted it as an obviously good suggestion they reminded me that the bread is plastic-wrapped and therefore has a four-day shelf life. They don't have any problem taking back one-day-old bread and selling it to their institutional customers. They will not suffer a loss even on week-old bread because they can sell that to a biscuit company for an even higher price than flour."

"Lovely, so that is the solution." I'm quite proud of myself.

"Efrat," he says as he releases another cloud through the window, "you haven't finished yet. What about the second question? How can we verify that the orders are still not too low? Remember, the inertia of the shops can cause them to still order less than the real demand."

That's easy. "Since leftovers don't create damage for the company, they just have to institute a procedure that when their driver sees that there are no leftovers from yesterday, he gives the shop a higher amount than he gave yesterday. If there are lots of leftovers he gives a little less. I'm sure that with some experience the practice can be rapidly established."

"Correct," he says. "Keep on."

Keep on? What else is there?

"Efrat, whenever you come up with a new solution you have to check all the ramifications, otherwise you might miss something important."

That I understand. But I still don't know what I'm supposed to do. To ensure that we'll have enough time, I turn to take the longer route. No risk of him noticing it.

He realizes that I'm stuck and he tries to help. "Will your suggestion eliminate the shop's conservatism?"

I give it another thought before I confidently answer, "It will."

Realizing that the clue he gave me didn't help, he

continues, grinning. "If that's the case, what is the point in switching from one delivery a day to two? One is enough. We'll get an even bigger increase than what we witnessed in the test and we'll not have to go through the trouble of two deliveries a day."

That's not what I'd expected. But it is so obvious, why am I surprised? Somehow I feel that it is important, so I keep digging into it.

His original solution, switching to replenishing twice a day, was a daring one. The test verified that it works excellently, beyond even the rosiest expectations. And now, without blinking an eye, he dumped it. Doesn't he have any inertia? And what about the fact that an inventor is supposed to fall in love with his inventions?

Is it uniqueness in Father's personality, or is what I witness now the true meaning of being deeply convinced that he doesn't know; the openness to rethink everything, including one's own good solutions, from scratch. I'm sure that to reach this level one has to practice for a very long time....

Father cuts into my thoughts. "Of course this didn't consume all three days. So we proceeded to construct an even better solution. I'm convinced that what we came up with, in terms of increasing the company's net profit, will dwarf whatever we've said so far."

This is the last thing I expected at this stage. But, in retrospect, this is the decisive example I was asking for. The company is about to realize record profits, much above the industry standards. This is definitely a very good situation. If he can come up with yet another solution, a solution that is so powerful that it will dwarf even what now seems possible, then I have to accept the possibility that any situation can be substantially improved.

"Father?" I ask, "when you look to improve a situation

that is not good I know your starting point. You start with the undesirable effects and dive down to find the core conflict. But what do you do when you start with a situation that is already good? Just turn your intuition loose?"

"Efrat, as I've told you again and again, I'm not a genius. I don't have the phenomenal intuition that is required for such a task."

"So how did you go about constructing the even better solution?"

"The hard way," he laughs. "As you pointed out, a good solution deals with the core conflict. It changes an underlying assumption and therefore significantly changes the situation. Then you face a reality that is very different from the reality you started with. Since the implementation of the solution is not yet complete, what we did was to first transfer ourselves into the future; to realize the situation that will exist after the company institutionalizes all the required changes. That is the hardest part. Efrat, do you want to try to do it? I'll help you."

"We're too close to home and I'm too curious," I answer. "I think you should just tell me."

"Okay. In this new situation, I was looking for the desirable effects, for the strong points the company will have. And there are many of them. The company will serve, through its own distribution warehouses and trucks, almost all the fast-moving-goods shops in their vast country, both in the towns and the rural areas. They will replenish to consumption. Which means that they will be able to demonstrate with hard numbers that for their products, their clients have unprecedented inventory turns coupled with exceptional sales per unit of shelf space. This also means that the company's sales force has excellent relationships with the shop owners.

Couple it with the fact that the switch to the mode of operation of replenishing-to-consumption frees up over three-quarters of the regional warehouse space. Now include the fact that a major part of their huge fleet, the trucks that deliver the bread, will be still standing idle for the majority of the day, and what do you get? You get the realization that selling and distributing additional Fast-Moving-Goods (FMG) could easily be done. Moreover, it could be done by the same infrastructure; it could be done without any meaningful increase in operating expenses."

"So you recommended they start to produce additional different products?"

"Not at all," he says as we enter our town. "That will require major investments in technology and production and will take a long time. If you noticed, their major advantages are in their better distribution and sales. Concentration on those advantages will lead to a better and faster way to capitalize on their excellent situation. Many brand companies, and I'm talking about many of the world giants, are not present in their country. These companies have already the best products, and not less important, they have the name recognition. Still, for them to enter directly into the company's country is a major investment in distribution and sales coupled with considerable risk. Don't you see how easy it is to construct fantastic win-win collaboration between the brand companies and our company?"

CHAPTER 14

Thinking Clearly
and Tautologies

Father and I are sitting in the backyard. It's a beautiful winter morning; one of those days that belong to the spring. He has a cup of coffee in his hand and his pipe is within reach. I'm stretched out on a comfy garden lounge chair with nothing in my hands; unlike him I don't need caffeine or nicotine to keep me going.

Today I'm determined to squeeze from Father the essence of thinking clearly. I've succeeded in dragging him out of his study, not a small achievement. I've disconnected all the phones in the house and I've even turned off my cell. Father doesn't have one. Mother and her sister have gone to south Tel Aviv, and my kids are in school. I will have three uninterrupted hours. That should be enough; at least for a start.

"Father," I say, "let me tell you what I accept, and what is still bothering me."

He stares at the dance of the sunspots below the trees, probably thinking about something else. That's okay. As I proceed I'll draw his attention. I am talking about things that are at the center of his life and I'm his favorite daughter, his only daughter.

"I fully agree that I don't want an easy life—I want a full life. I also accept that in order to live a full life I have to have enough good opportunities and I need to advance some of these opportunities to a level where I'll feel I have made significant achievements."

He doesn't react but that doesn't slow me down. "By watching and listening to you I think I'm convinced that rather than leaving it to chance—to what people call good luck—my chances of living a full life will be much greater if I learn to think clearly. I'll be able to generate, or at least to recognize, the right opportunities for me, and I'll be better able and have more stamina to persistently follow enough of them to fruition."

I still don't get any sign of interest. "You claim that the only things standing in the way of me thinking clearly are some specific obstacles."

"Obstacles and practice. A lot of practice."

At last, some reaction. A little provocation is in place to get this discussion rolling. In a slightly stronger tone I say, "That is exactly my problem. You say that to think clearly, to think like a true scientist, a lot of practice is needed. I think that I am thinking constantly, whether I'm conscious of it or not. But that is apparently not what you mean by practice, so will you please tell me how one practices thinking clearly?"

In a surprised voice, still gazing at the sunspots, he says, "Isn't it evident when one makes sense and when one just wastes time babbling."

I'm not going to let him brush it away. "Can you give me a clear definition of the difference?" I persist.

Quite indifferently he answers, "The key to thinking clearly is to avoid circular logic, that's all."

"Father," I say in a firm tone, "can we discuss it? It is important for me to really understand it." At last, he looks directly at me. After a short time he says in a soft voice, "Sorry, Daughter."

He lights his pipe, thinks while releasing some clouds of smoke, and after a short while, starts. "As we have said, everything is connected through cause-and-effect relationships, and at the bottom there are only a few elements. So the key to thinking clearly is to build logical maps. You start with an effect, any effect, and dive down to the root causes by asking, 'why does the effect exist?' The difficulty is that when we dive down, sooner or later we reach causes that are entities, the existence of which cannot be verified directly through our senses; we reach abstract entities."

"Clarify please," I say, trying to slow him down.

He smiles and continues more slowly. "In the hard sciences, when we dive down asking why that exists, after some iterations we reach depths where we can no longer use our senses and we have to start using abstract entities."

"Abstract entities?"

"Entities like atoms or enzymes. Has anybody ever seen an atom or an enzyme? Has anybody talked to them or touched one? They probably do exist, but we know it through logic and not through the direct information of our senses."

I never thought about it this way, but it is obviously correct. Gladly I say, "Good thing that I chose the social sciences so I don't have to deal with such intangible speculations. In high school I felt uncomfortable with atoms, and then the science teacher started to talk about even more abstract things like protons and neutrons. Now I hear that they are talking about elementary particles and quarks. I'm better off dealing with tangible things like people."

He smiles. "Daughter, I'm afraid that if you are feeling uncomfortable with abstract entities you have chosen the wrong profession. When we deal with people, often with the first attempt to dive down to a cause, we encounter such abstract entities." Without waiting for my response he explains, "For example, take the last case we were discussing. Did you ever see or touch 'conservatism'? We come to realize that conservatism exists not because we witness it directly via our senses but because we deduce its existence through our logic."

Come to think about it, almost everything that psychology deals with, like love or hate, like motivation or intelligence, are things the existence of which we deduce through our logic. For Father they must be as intangible as atoms or quarks.

"What is the importance of these 'abstract entities' in thinking clearly?" I ask.

"It's important to be careful because it is so easy to end up in la-la land when dealing with entities that cannot be verified by direct observation. It is so easy to fall into the trap of circular logic; of tautologies. And then the road to sophisticated nonsense is wide open. Efrat, do you know what tautologies are?"

"I can recite the example you gave me about the planets moving in circles, but frankly I need to understand it better in order to relate it to daily life."

"We are surrounded by tautologies," he states, "to the extent that we are insensitive to them. They appear in almost every conversation and in almost any article in the newspapers. Take for example a sentence like, 'They lost the game because they didn't have enough motivation to win.' And in the rest of the article there is no shred of direct evidence that the team didn't have enough motivation. Now ask yourself, 'Why do we accept it? How do we know that the team didn't have enough motivation?' And the answer most likely is, 'They lost the game, didn't they?' A tautology."

I smile but have to say, "I don't believe I frequently use such nonsense arguments. At least not when it's important."

"Oh, you don't?" And grinning, he raises his eyes to the treetops and says, "Some psychologist, not too long ago, told me, 'You don't feel disappointment because you repress your disappointment.' I didn't bother to ask,

'How do you know that I repress my disappointment?' Because the answer would be, 'Isn't it obvious? I know that you repress your disappointment because you don't feel disappointed.' A circular argument."

After delivering this cheap shot he continues, "Circular logic is a point of no return for thinking clearly. You use it once and from then on you are blocked from diving down to the root cause, and instead you are building castles on quicksand. The problem is that circular logic sounds right, and when we cannot check it directly we tend to accept it as a given. Efrat, just realize how convinced you were that I do repress my feelings when actually you didn't have any evidence to support it."

I think about it. Finally I ask, "So how can one avoid using circular logic?"

"Let me first enlarge your base of understanding."

"That is an excellent idea," I encourage him. Having majored in psychology I wasn't required to take even a single course in logic. Why does Father expect me to know it all? Probably because he regards logic as a basic ability of an intelligent person, as basic as the ability to express oneself clearly. Viewing it from this aspect he might be right. I force myself to stop thinking about it and concentrate on what he is saying.

He is already talking full speed. "Let me emphasize that circular logic doesn't imply that the cause given for the effect is wrong, it just states that contrary to first impression the causality was not substantiated." Seeing that I have a problem he hurries to give an example. "Sales of our products are declining because the market taste is changing. If I leave it as is, this sentence is another fine example of a tautology."

"Yes, it is. And as I'm becoming sensitive to tautologies I must say that they are not convincing. I can come up with many other 'becauses' besides 'the market taste is changing.' It might be that sales are declining because there is a downturn in the economy, or because there is new competition, or because our service deteriorated or because we raised our prices. There are so many plausible causes, and with the information we have been given there is no reason to prefer one of them over the others."

"Now you are thinking." He is apparently pleased. "Now suppose that I tell you that I verified the existence of another effect: the sales of alternative products increased by about the same amount. What do you now think about the validity of the claim that the cause for both effects is that the market taste is changing?"

It is unlikely that the increase in the alternative products and the comparable decrease in our products is just a coincidence. Aloud I say, "Now a change in market taste is the only plausible explanation that I can think of. I still don't know what the cause is for the cause; I don't know why the market taste changed. It could be that we caused it by lowering our service or by increasing our price. It might not be connected to anything we did, but to external forces. To decipher that, more information is needed. But I do accept that our sales' decline is due to a market change in taste. It is common sense. But, Father, you brought the second effect from thin air. How am I going to do it?"

"We'll come to it once you have a better understanding of the foundation," he assures me. "So, what we now realize is that whenever one uses circular logic the causality is not substantiated, and to make sense—common sense—things must be substantiated. To substantiate a cause, at a minimum, another resulting effect is needed; an effect that is verified by direct observation. Moreover, once the cause is substantiated you are not facing a dead end, instead your mind is racing to figure out the deeper cause. You are diving down for the root cause."

To that I agree.

"Now we are ready to address your concern that you might have difficulty coming up with a second resulting effect. First let me acknowledge that you have a base for that concern, because finding a second resulting effect requires thinking out of the box, the box we put ourselves in by concentrating on the original effect and the cause we speculated for its existence. Taking the last example, to come up with the second effect one must enlarge the scope from concentrating on just our products to encompass also the alternative products that might be very different from ours."

I try to digest. "The difficulty is that if I'm not sure, really sure, that a second effect does exist, I might stay inside the box; it is always safer to stay within the comfortable boundaries of a box than to jump out into the unknown. Since the other effect is not within that box, I will not find it. I'll give up searching and remain stuck with a tautology."

"Correct." Father is pleased. "And your last observation highlights why Inherent Simplicity is so helpful. Inherent Simplicity recognizes that as we dive down, causes converge. Convergence means that each meaningful cause is responsible not for just one effect, but for more than one. Believing in Inherent Simplicity assures us that for any meaningful cause there are at least two different effects."

"I see."

He continues, "And you are also right in pointing out that usually we don't know where to look once outside of the box. The fact that we needed a person of Newton's caliber to open our eyes to the convergence indicates that, in many cases—as long as we don't recognize the common cause—the effects look to us as though they have nothing in common; that they belong to different situations or time frames. The belief in Inherent Simplicity gives the assurance that at least one more effect exists, we just have to enlarge the scope we are looking at in order to find it. Most people have enough intuition, and together with this assurance, after some practice, they are able to easily come up with additional effects to verify, or refute, a claimed cause. Inherent Simplicity opens the door to verifying an abstract entity."

As much as I appreciate people's intuition I think that Father expects too much. The straw that breaks my back is the word "easily." But regarding Father's deep belief that every person has powerful intuition, I know that openly expressing my disbelief will irritate him. In a gentle voice I say, "Since you opened the door, will you please escort me in? Can you show me real cases where you used it?"

"No problem, I used it on every case I'm thinking about. But shall I first summarize it for you?" he asks.

That's exactly what I need. "Please do."

"You asked how one practices thinking clearly. Here is the answer. Efrat, to practice you don't choose a subject and free up the time to do a full analysis. That is not the right approach. You should use any opportunity to try and decipher the cause and effect. Be it a casual conversation with a stranger, a comment from your husband, or something that you are reading. You said that you are constantly thinking, and you are right, but that implies that you should try to constantly think clearly."

"Makes sense," I agree.

"So, whenever you hear or read a 'because,' and especially when the cause contains an abstract entity, be on guard. Even if the claim is expressed in total confidence you should not accept it as correct. Don't even accept the abstract entity itself as a fact of life. You should recognize it as just a hypothesis, or in other words, a guess. Now you proceed to try and come up with a predicted effect, with another effect that must be the result of the same cause. Remember, if you can't figure it out—if you can't find another effect—it is not because there are no other resulting effects, but because you think too narrowly. And to keep you straight, check that the predicted effect you come up with can be verified by direct observation, and take the time to verify it. The more predicted effects verified, the higher the validity of the cause. The more you practice the easier it becomes." Smiling, he adds, "When you practice it to the extent that it becomes second nature to you, people might start calling you a genius."

"Not to worry," I respond. "Between my work, the house and the kids I will never get enough practice because I will never have enough time to test the predicted effects."

"Oops," he says. "I'm afraid that I gave you the wrong impression. In the vast majority of cases it doesn't take more than a second or two."

"Really?" I'm pleasantly surprised.

Father smiles. "It does require us to check the existence of the predicted effects but that doesn't necessarily mean that we have to always launch tests. Just check, most times the existence of the predicted effect is already known to us."

Far from being convinced, I say, "I could use an example."

"Just try it. Already the first case, or maximum the second, will show you that I'm right."

I just keep looking at him.

He sighs. "Okay, if you insist." After sucking on his pipe he continues, "We can avoid wasting time by taking an example that will also highlight the extent to which we don't use our brain and instead accept idiotic tautologies just because everybody believes in them. Moreover, it will help me demonstrate the extent to which we are jumping carelessly to conclusions about people's behavior." He winks at me, asking, "Have you heard the phrase 'People resist change—the bigger the change, the bigger the resistance'?"

Smiling, I answer, "I wish I had a nickel for each time I've heard it. So what about it?"

"Put it within the context it is usually said and you'll be able to smell the ugly odor of a tautology."

In a deep pompous voice I say, "We are facing difficulties implementing XYZ because people resist change."

He smiles. "That is a pretty good imitation, done with all the confidence and authority of a consultant or a manager. But this statement includes the word 'because' and the cause contains an abstract entity. Which means that one should not accept it without thinking. Well, let's hear how you do the thinking."

I'm not yet proficient in coming up with predicted effects so I move carefully. "What do we mean by 'people resist change'? Since this statement does not contain any qualifications, it actually states that people resist almost any change under almost any circumstances. If that is the case people will certainly avoid initiating and actively pursuing changes that will transform their lifestyle—a predicted effect."

"Good," he encourages me. "Now be more specific. What are the biggest changes in a person's life? I mean besides being born and dying."

It is easy to proceed. "Many people are looking forward eagerly to getting married or having a baby. Changes that, from firsthand experience I know, alter almost every aspect of life. Yes, no one jumps into such changes without some level of hesitation, but judging

ELIYAHU M. GOLDRATT

from the behavior and attitude of so many of my friends it definitely cannot be described as resisting change. Just the opposite."

I'm thinking about when people do resist change, trying to formulate the needed qualifications, when Father says, "Efrat, I can hear the wheels turning at full speed in your head. Slow down. The first reason I raised the subject of resistance to change was to enable you to answer your question. 'Where are you going to get the time to verify the predicted effects?' Will you concentrate on that and try to verbalize your conclusions? Start with something along the lines of, 'Father, you are right.' In many cases the predicted effects do not require us to spend a lot of time launching a test because from our general experience we already know whether or not they exist."

I'm not going to give him that satisfaction. Instead I say sweetly, "You forgot to mention that the process of coming up with a predicted effect may lead to the invalidation of the hypothesis. Actually, to the realization that the hypothesis was embarrassingly wrong, or at the very least, inaccurate."

"Correct," he confirms. "That is the basis of science as was formulated by Karl Popper. In science, every claim, every hypothesis, every cause is considered to be relevant only if it can be put to the test. A test that potentially is capable of disproving the claim. Otherwise we are not talking about science but pseudoscience; about witchcraft. And yes, Daughter, more often than not, once we come up with a predicted effect we realize that it doesn't exist and therefore the hypothesis is wrong. You may come up with ten predicted effects that turn out to exist, and then you think a little more and you come up with the eleventh predicted effect that doesn't exist and that single one is enough to shatter the valid-

126

ity of the proposed cause. The more predicted effects verified, the higher the validity of the cause, but there is always the possibility that tomorrow will bring yet another predicted effect and that one will turn out not to exist. We can never be sure that something is absolutely true."

I think I get it. "You made your point," I assure him.

"Not yet, darling. I'm far from making it yet. There is another lesson I want you to learn from the last example. I want you to realize how careless we are in relating derogatory characteristics and intentions to people."

Where is that coming from?

Responding to my surprised expression he asks, "What actually is implied by a statement like 'people resist change'? Does it imply good things about people's personalities? Don't you realize that it actually claims that people are programmed to resist, irrespective of the content of the proposed change? That claim certainly doesn't give too much credit to people's judgment. It is a derogatory statement."

There is thunder in his voice when he continues. "And this claim is accepted by almost everyone, even though it doesn't take more than a few minutes to examine the evidence that is all around us; the evidence that leads to the conclusion that this claim is, at best, inaccurate. What do you think about that subject?"

"Only that people protect their interests and they are very good at doing that."

"I meant, what do you think about our culture? A culture that has no hesitation assuming derogatory things about people. Actually it encourages it."

I just make a face.

He is apparently not satisfied with my response. "Never think that we are not influenced by it; we are an integral part of that culture. We had better recognize that in a situation that involves people, whenever our intuition is searching for a cause, there is a high likelihood that it will come up with a hypothesis that is derogatory to people. And our intuition will surface in our mind only the predicted effects that will validate that false hypothesis, while screening out all the other predicted effects that disprove it. If you are not careful to guard against this tendency, your chances of doing a meaningful analysis are very slim."

"Father, I think that I see people as they are and I'm extremely careful not to raise, not even in my mind, unsubstantiated derogatory accusations. Give me some credit."

Father is not happy. He stands up and starts to pace, releasing clouds of smoke like an old locomotive. I don't move. Finally he stops and asks, "Efrat, will you, at least, be willing to test yourself?"

"What is the test?"

"There was a case that puzzled me for a long time. A group of people behaved in a way that I couldn't understand. Do you mind reading about that case and do your best to try to come up with plausible causes that can explain that group's strange behavior?"

"That's all? I'll be delighted to do it."

He stands up. "Let me send you the report."

CHAPTER 15

Comfort Zones*

Have you ever classified people as open-minded or con-servative? What about action-oriented people or pro-crastinators? After thirty years of trying to induce orga-nizations to change, such classifications are so deeply ingrained in my thinking that they do have major ramifi-cations on my actions. I tend to decide early on whether or not I would like to work with a company based on the classification box I had slotted the top management into. This audit visit forced me to realize that that clas-sification might lead to grave mistakes. Let me describe what brought me to such a radical conclusion.

The company is producing fast-moving consumer goods (FMCG) in India. (Toothpaste is a fast-moving consumer good, while an electric toothbrush is not.) I am speci-fying the country because most people who have not done business in India (like me until three years ago) do

---

*This report was written and circulated to the Goldratt Group in Feb-ruary 2007. For the purpose of this book it was slightly modified to enable easy reading for readers who are not familiar with the Theory of Constraints.

not comprehend the scale of this country. I think it will suffice to highlight that in India the number of FMCG shops is 6.5 million. No, this is not a typo. The number of this type of shop in India is more than the number of people living in my country, infants included. Our company is a medium player; it has close to ten percent of the market. Still, in the vast Indian market that means that they are selling their products through two thousand distributors serving 2.5 million shops.

Their eagerness to grow drove them to the dangerous situation where instead of taking the time to open the bottleneck, they took the shortcut of buying forty percent of their intermediate product from the outside.[*]

To rectify the situation it is vital to find ways to increase the bottleneck production. Using the standard techniques of TOC, those already described in *The Goal*, within six weeks from the beginning of the project and without any significant investment, the situation was reversed in all four of their plants. Instead of buying this intermediate product, they started selling their intermediate product to other manufacturers.

Without losing a beat, they moved to the next step in the improvement plan. Like so many companies that have both production and distribution, this company did not have a plant warehouse—everything that was produced

---

[*]To understand how dangerous this situation can be, consider a company that produces car engines. The crucial element in an engine is the cylinders. Now imagine that there is a bottleneck in cylinder production that limits the number of cylinders the company can produce and therefore the number of engines it can sell. A shortcut would be to buy 40% of cylinders from their competitor. Taking this shortcut, the company is now at the mercy of its competitor.

was shipped the same day to one of about thirty regional warehouses. Since the future demand for each SKU at each warehouse is not precisely known, that practice led to having too much inventory in one warehouse while not having enough at another warehouse. Cross shipments between warehouses were the norm. They were moving at such a pace that before long, the new plant warehouses were in place and were stocked with the right amount of inventories for each one of their close to a hundred SKUs. Since the plants have some overlapping capabilities, the plants' warehouses were managed as one logical warehouse.

Then they moved to the next link; they implemented the replenishment-to-consumption mode of operation to control shipments from the plant warehouse to all their regional warehouses. As you know, this is not just a matter of modifying a computer system; it requires the much more difficult and sensitive challenge of changing managers' span of authority. The regional warehouse managers no longer call the shots; they are no longer placing orders from the plants. Rather, the system replenishes the regional warehouse automatically according to the shipments from each regional warehouse to the distributors. Also, the warehouse managers no longer decide on the target levels of inventories in their regional warehouse. Rather, the target inventory levels are decided and constantly monitored by the system. The responsibility of the regional warehouse manager is now restricted to properly managing the operations of the warehouse.

Inventories went down and shortages were almost eliminated. The real robustness of the system was vividly demonstrated to the entire company a few months after completion of that step. In the monsoon, a flood damaged most of the goods held in one of the regional warehouses. In the past, such a misfortune would have caused major disruptions in supply in that region. The regional warehouse manager wrote a memo stating that the disruptions were surprisingly small and that within one week everything was back to normal.

All of the above, and a resulting increase of about ten percent in sales, was achieved in slightly less than five months from the beginning of the improvement project. How would you classify the managers of this company? Would you classify them as open-minded and action-oriented, as results-driven? I personally think that in this case such adjectives might not be strong enough.

But that is not the end of the story. The next step, as you all know, was to expand the replenishment-to-consumption mode of operations from internal distribution (plant warehouse to regional warehouses) into external distribution (from the regional warehouses to the distributors). That's when the first signs of hesitation appeared.

The distributors are not employees of the company; each distributor is a separate independent business. Now consider the meaning of approaching a distributor and suggesting that they switch to this particular replenishment-to-consumption solution. One way of looking at it is that we have to go to a distributor and tell him, "Dear friend, today, as the business owner, you determine what we should ship to you; you are placing the orders. We suggest that from tomorrow on, you will report to us, on a daily basis, what you have sold, and we will be the ones who decide what we'll ship to you and, as a consequence, we will also determine how much inventory you will hold."

What is the anticipated reaction of a distributor to such an offer? Most likely it will be in the form of rhetorical questions like, "Are you serious?! Are you suggesting that you know how to run my business better than I do?!"

This was certainly the anticipation of the sales managers, especially when they considered the company's track record of missed shipments and the constant pressure of trying to push inventories on the distributors. No wonder that there was a level of hesitance and of skepticism that the distributors would agree to the company's proposal.

The company's sales force was properly prepared. The win-win nature of the replenishment solution was highlighted (the win for the company and the win for the distributors). The sales force was engaged in constructing the buy-in presentations. Extensive role-playing was done. The sixty-eight largest distributors were chosen as the target for the initial effort, which was launched and completed in May 2005. To the astonishment of the sales force, all sixty-eight distributors accepted the offer (with varying degrees of enthusiasm). The following few weeks were tense for the top managers of the company since the sales of their products to the sixty-eight major distributors dropped sharply (while the surplus inventories the distributors were holding were flushed out). Then, sales went up and continued to creep up. Everyone was breathing normally again. Until the end of 2005, the replenishment initiative was extended to encompass an additional five hundred distributors—now covering over sixty-five percent of the sales of the company. The sales increase, relative to the previous year, was about thirty percent—much higher than the market growth.

Let's do an intermediate summary. We know that when production is improved it does have a positive impact on availability and therefore on sales. We know that holding the inventories in a plant warehouse, rather than pushing them to the regional warehouses, further improves availability. We know that putting the internal, and more so the external, distribution on the replenishment-to-consumption solution brings the availability from the distributors to almost perfect levels. The impact of all those improvements combined led to about a thirty percent increase in sales, an increase that was not associated with any increase in expenses or investments. (The small investment needed for improving the plant's capacity and the larger investment needed for the plant warehouse's inventory were more than compensated for by the much bigger reduction in the inventories in the regional warehouses.) The company was making record profits and the managers got record bonuses.

But, as you know, that is not the end of the road. Whatever was accomplished that far was just paving the way for the next step. The most powerful improvement, in terms of increasing sales and profits, is to extend replenishment to the retailers. This is the most powerful step due to two main reasons. One reason is that variability is the highest at the retail level, and as a result, in retail the shortages are the highest. A distributor, and more so the company warehouses, experience less variability due to the impact of aggregation. Eliminating the shortages at the retail level will therefore result in the highest increase in sales. The second reason is that the pressure of limited shelf space and cash is the highest at the retail level, and as a result, a shop is holding a relatively low percentage of the available SKUs; a typical small shop holds about five SKUs (in India a small shop is really small) and a regular shop holds about ten to twenty SKUs out of the close to one hundred SKUs available.

The replenishment solution, once it reaches the shops, reduces the shortages while reducing inventories. The higher the frequency of replenishment, the higher the impact—increasing frequency of delivery from once a week to once a day practically eliminates shortages while reducing inventories to considerably less than half. Such a drastic reduction of inventory, and the realization that the company's products sell very well relative to the investment in cash and space, induces the shops to extend the range of products they hold. Considerably fewer shortages, coupled with offering many more SKUs per shop, has a major impact on increasing sales.

The improvements in just the previous links of the supply chain had already yielded a thirty percent increase in sales. We were looking forward to the next decisive step—extending our solution to retail—a step that is expected to at least double that increase in sales. That would be the tipping point of the implementation.

Let me elaborate on the last sentence. Suppose the conservative prediction that extending the replenishment to retail will only result in an additional thirty percent increase in sales. The improvements in the plant's capacity can easily sustain the combined sixty percent increase in sales without adding any additional expenses. The total-variable-cost of the company's products constitute about sixty percent of the sales' prices; the throughput is forty percent of sales. That means that, at that stage of the implementation, the net profit of the company will be increased by (0.6x0.4=) more than twenty percent of the previous sales. Before the improvement project, the company's net profit was slightly above the average for its industry, about six percent on sales. Now it is expected to reach twenty percent profit on sales, a level of performance never heard of before in that industry. Imagine what a positive impact it will have on the morale of the employees and the confidence of the shareholders.

But to see the real impact, we have to examine the impact these improvements have on the other links of the company's supply chain and, as a result, on the tangible opportunities that will open up.

The distributors already enjoy an increase of thirty percent in sales associated with about a forty percent decrease in inventory. The further increase in sales due to extending replenishment to the shops will not cause any meaningful increase in inventories the distributors will have to hold since the frequency of shipments to the shops will be increased (and by that, smoothing the demand from the distributors). The prime measurement of the distributors is inventory turns; an improvement of ten percent in inventory turns is regarded as very good news. The inventory turns of the distributors will be improved by (1.6/0.6=) over 250%! That fantastic increase guarantees that the company will not have any problems attracting the vast number of new distributors required to cover the rest of the Indian market (expanding the reach of the company from 2.5 million shops to the existing 6.5 million). That expansion will again meaningfully increase the sales and profits of the company.

The real, unlimited potential is revealed when we examine the impact that extending the replenishment solution has on retail. Does our solution have any impact on retail? At first glance, it seems unlikely since the company's products constitute less than five percent of a shop's sales.

What about giving it a second glance? The large stores that sell mainly FMCG are the supermarkets. Maybe you are not aware of the fact that two percent profits on sales are considered very good for supermarkets in the western world; the markup of the supermarkets on FMCG is about fifteen to thirty-five percent but the net profit is much smaller due to the expenses, and more so due to the inherent conceptual ineffectiveness of the prevailing mode of operation.

Don't have too much pity for supermarkets. Considering the large sales volumes and the relatively small investments, two-percent profit on sales makes supermarkets a very good business. The markup of a small shop in India is less than the markup of supermarkets in the western world, the expenses are much smaller, and the conceptual mode of operation and therefore the ineffectiveness, are the same. The combined effect is that most small shops in India make slightly less than one-percent net profit on sales.

Considering such tiny profit percentages and realizing that the shops' sales are composed of the sales of many types of products, each representing at most just a few percent of sales, the shop owners of small stores are extremely sensitive to which products are selling well and which are not, and act accordingly. In large stores, the prime measurement that guides which product will get more shelf space and which will be dropped is sales/shelf. An increase of fifty percent in sales of the company's products, an increase that is not associated with increasing inventory or shelf space, is bound to elevate them to the top of the favorite products of the shops, big and small.*

A shop experiencing such a positive impact from selling our company's products will certainly welcome offerings of other products of the company. Especially if the company chooses products on which the shops traditionally have higher markups. The expansion of the replenishment offer to the shops opens wide the possibility to streamline new products to the market. Only the future will show how well-utilized was the opportunity to harvest the impact (on the company's future sales and profits) of easy introduction of new products capitalizing on its impressive distribution and sales capabilities.

In November 2005, I was disappointed to find out that no effort was yet taken to continue to the next link of the supply chain: the retail. Considering that at that stage I was already spoiled by the go-getter attitude of this

---

*It is important to note that, for all practical purposes, the competitors cannot counter this. To emulate what our company is doing is very difficult. Read on to see the enormous psychological barriers that are standing in the way. For the competitors to react in the quick traditional way of rebates, gifts, or a plain reduction in price is also impossible, as can be clearly deduced by the following calculation. Assume that our company's products represent as low as 2% of the shops sales and the accumulated increase in sales was only 60%. Further suppose a low margin of the shops, just 10%. For a competitor to match our impact on the shop's profitability he will have to decrease his prices to the shop by 6%, practically wiping out all of his profits.

company, you can imagine my frustration at witness-
ing apparent procrastination. No wonder that as 2006
drifted along and still no efforts were initiated to seriously approach the retailers, I started to put some gentle, and then less gentle, pressure. What we faced can be
described as paralysis. Actually, considering the number
and intensity of the reservations that were raised to support the argument that there is no point in approaching
the shops with the replenishment offer, the attitude can
be better described as "active paralysis." If such a phrase
does not exist, it sure needs to.

What caused such a drastic change in behavior?

I pondered this question for a long time. On one hand,
all my experience leads me to believe that there are
people who are more open-minded than others. On the
other hand, characterizing people as open-minded people or conservative people, as action-oriented people or
procrastinators, will lead to the ridiculous conclusion
that the managers of the company all went through an
almost instant transformation.

CHAPTER 16

People Are Good

What are the plausible causes that can explain that group's behavior? To really test myself I deliberately erase from my mind Father's warning, and rather concentrate on the first thoughts that pop up. The managers of this company are now on top of the world; they already brought their company to performance that is considerably higher than anybody else in their industry. They got hefty bonuses. Everybody is praising their achievements. Maybe they'd had enough?

Especially when the proposed next step involves a mammoth effort; launching an untraditional offer to 2.5 million shops is a daunting task. Moreover, who guarantees them that it will work at all? Who guarantees that it will lead to a significant increase in sales? Better to play it safe.

Besides, one cannot compare the business smarts of an owner of a distribution center—a person who turns a considerable amount of money every month, who is familiar with financial statements and computerized systems—to the owners of small shops; people who may not even have a computer. The vast majority of small-shop owners probably never heard the term "inventory turns." What is the chance that they will understand the offer and be willing to collaborate with it? It is no wonder that the managers of that company stuck their heels in the ground and refused to continue to the next step.

What will be Father's reaction to my reading of the situation?

He will tear it to pieces.

I claim that they don't move because they don't want to risk their good situation. Father will highlight that this hypothesis doesn't stand the test of predicted effects. When the project started, the company was in a good situation; their net profit was above the industry standard. Managers who don't want to risk a good situation are not likely to change procedures and policies that they followed for decades; procedures and policies that brought them to be a successful company. But the facts are that they enthusiastically changed the way they were guiding production, that they did change dramatically the internal and external mode of distribution. And they made all those changes in less than one year. I cannot claim that they just paused to allow the system to stabilize. The system was humming already at the end of 2005, and not moving for an additional year cannot be called "just paused."

But the next step is much more risky.

I can vividly hear the cynicism in his questions. Is it? In what way is it more risky? It was a risk to invest in building the plant warehouses. It was a risk to allow all the major distributors to flush out their inventories. What is the risk in approaching, let's say, one thousand shops out of 2.5 million and seeing their reaction to the company's new offer?

And what about the mammoth efforts to convince and handle 2.5 million shops? That cannot be compared to handling just thirty regional warehouses or even two thousand distributors. It is a task that is a thousand times bigger.

I can see the smile spreading on his face. "Efrat," he will say, "for you a number like two-and-a-half million is scary, but this is their day in and day out reality. They are currently servicing those shops and they, of course, have the proper infrastructure to handle it. Just ask yourself, what is the difference between what we asked them to do, and launching a promotion, something that they routinely do?"

Good thing I played all of it out in my head. I saved myself a major embarrassment. To categorize these managers as risk avoiders, especially when the next step involves almost no risk, is ridiculous.

But, the important thing is that I think I learned my lesson. The first causes that jumped into my mind were derogatory, were unsubstantiated, and regarding the enormous potential of the next step, these causes were actually accusations. I feel uneasy when I recall what I thought about the shops' owners. I ignored the vast experience I have bargaining with owners of small shops and ending up holding the short side of the stick. These people don't have business smarts? They will not be able to grasp the win for them in our offer? Nonsense.

If it weren't for the fact that I know that I will have to justify my answer to Father; if it weren't for the fact that I know how he is going to analyze it, I might have accepted my speculated causes as truth. Where would it have left me? In a situation where I would be convinced that there is no point in continuing to push them to pro-ceed to the next step. I would lower, substantially, my expectations of what can be achieved and I would do it for no good reason. Moreover, I would be even more convinced in my skepticism about people.

Maybe Father is right. Maybe our perception of

people's behavior should be reexamined. I started to think about it awhile ago, when I realized the extent to which we tend to blame people when we are involved in conflicts that do not have an acceptable compromise. But now I realize that the tendency to blame people is stretching much beyond the situations where we are personally involved in a conflict. Here is a case that I was not involved in. There is no apparent conflict and nevertheless my tendency to blame, to bring up unsubstantiated derogatory "explanations" blinded me to the extent that I was about to give up on an excellent opportunity to achieve incredible improvements.

I know what Father will say, I've heard him pondering it for as long as I remember. The keys to thinking clearly are the belief in Inherent Simplicity and, not less important, the belief that people are not bad. A belief that leads to the practice that every hypothesis, before it is even entertained as a plausible hypothesis, should first pass the test of not being derogatory.

Until now I just dismissed it. As a psychologist I know that there is a debate over the nature of people. Some, including Freud, claim that people are born bad. Others claim that people are born as a tabula rasa and they might become bad due to environmental influence. How can I seriously entertain the opinion that people are good? More than half of my professional training was on cases where people behaved in a way that is certainly not good.

On the other hand, Father's approach is pragmatic and it does work. If I want to improve my chances of living a full life I'd better learn how to think clearly. And to do that I must overcome the obstacle of my tendency to seek refuge in blaming others; raising derogatory explanations. Now that I'm much more alert to the magnitude of that obstacle and how devastating it is, maybe I should rethink my opinions about people's behavior.

I'll think about it some other time. Right now I want to figure out a real cause that could explain those managers strange behavior. I'm an organizational psychologist; I should be able to come up with a good answer.

What can explain the difference in their behavior in the first stages of the implementation as compared to the last stage? Is there a difference in the stages themselves? The first few stages required major changes in their company and the companies they are intimately dealing with—an environment that they are very familiar with. Maybe these managers do not continue to move because the next step requires them to go out of their comfort zone?

This looks like a good direction. But I don't fool myself. As long as I don't fully understand what I'm talking about, all I'm doing is hiding behind pompous, professional terminology.

I wish I hadn't accepted Father's test. But since I did, I have to continue to think before I cave in and read his suggested solution.

CHAPTER 17

Comfort Zones
(Continued)

A plausible explanation might be provided by the widespread opinion that people's behavior is dependent on their comfort zones; when people are operating within their comfort zone you can expect open minds and action; when they are pushed outside their comfort zone, expect hesitance and resistance.

Personally, it is not easy for me to accept such an explanation, not without a precise definition of the term 'comfort zone,' not without a clear description of the mechanism that connects comfort zone to attitudes.

What is a comfort zone?

It is customary to think that a comfort zone is an area where a person feels that he has control, or at least a sufficient amount of influence. That can explain the behavior of our company's management. As long as they addressed their own operation, an area where they have full control, they moved like blue lightning. Once they had to go out of the company's boundaries, to the distributors, the first signs of hesitation appeared. Still, since the arrangement with the distributors is based on exclusivity—the distributors store and sell only the products of our company—the management of the company felt they had sufficient influence over their distributors, and they moved (first cautiously and then aggressively). But when it reached retail—where the products of the company constitute only a small fraction of a shop's sales—the management of the company felt that they certainly didn't have any control or even sufficient influence, and that is when their behavior changed.

Even though the above explanation does fit all the facts that we saw in this company, it also indicates that unless we find a way to have some level of effective control or influence over retail, management will continue to drag their feet. That prediction is in direct conflict with what I have witnessed in so many other situations. Take, for example, the common situation of a manufacturer of parts that are sold to another manufacturer. In most such cases, there are plenty of competitors, and the parts that are sold represent a small fraction of the client purchases, which means that, definitely, the supplier doesn't have any effective control or influence over its clients. Still, in most such cases, we didn't have major difficulty convincing the suppliers to approach their clients with a radically untraditional offer.

To fit all the facts, those that were observed in this company and those that have been observed in manufacturers of parts, examine the opinion that a comfort zone has less to do with control and more to do with knowledge. Suppose that a comfort zone is defined as a zone where a person feels that he has sufficient knowledge of cause and effect; of what is going to be the likely outcome of an action; of what is going to be the likely response to a suggestion.*

---

*Such knowledge does lead to the ability to effectively influence the situation and therefore it is no wonder that comfort zones are associated with control and influence.

According to this definition, pushing a person outside his comfort zone is describing the following scenario:

1. A suggestion is raised (pushed) to take a specific action in order to reach a specific desirable effect.

2. The person, based on his knowledge of the relevant cause and effect, is convinced that the suggested action cannot cause, or has a small chance to cause, the desirable effect.

According to the above definition it is obvious that we should expect resistance when the person is seeing different cause and effect than we use. How much resistance? Well, it depends on what led our clients to believe in their existing cause and effect. I now believe that we better distinguish between two different types of situations—one where people have experience and the other where people do not.

The first type is when we try to convince people to change rooted ways of behavior they have practiced for decades, like the changes we suggested to the managers of this company regarding their production and distribution. In the past we regarded these cases as the most difficult ones to change. I don't think so anymore. Not that they are easy, but the other type is much more difficult.

In the first type of situation, the cause-and-effect connections of our clients were based on enormous experience. The flaws they had in some of their cause-and-effect connections stemmed not from lack of experience, but from the fact that they were operating under a wrong paradigm. Usually their previous paradigm stemmed from one way or another of exercising local optima. The mere fact that our suggestion is based on causes and effects that are taken from another paradigm means that by raising our suggestion we do push our clients outside their comfort zone. To fully realize it, imagine the reaction of our clients if we were to present the needed actions without any explanation. Would anybody follow our suggestions and implement these changes? Not a chance!

This is the reason that in those cases we are careful to first explain the logic of the new paradigm and assist them in using their vast experience to validate it. The fact that they do have a lot of relevant experience helps us in two ways. The first one, as we said, is that they can use their experience to quickly verify and embrace the "new" cause and effect. The second is that their experience helps them with the fine details that are needed to fully adjust our suggestions to fit their specific circumstances.

That is not the case in the second type of situation we might witness in a Viable Vision implementation—situations where our suggested actions relate to an area where they do not have any firsthand experience. In such a situation their cause-and-effect connections are based on extrapolation from areas where they do have a lot of experience, and that extrapolation might be flawed; in extreme cases such extrapolation might not even be relevant.

An example of the less extreme case is when we asked the company to extend the replenishment mode of operation to the distributors. The managers' experience is based on the reality of their company, a reality in which inventory turns are not regarded as a crucial measurement; they are just one of the many measurements used. Extrapolating from that experience to the distributors' environment—where inventory turns are the prime operational measurement—led to the prediction that not passing control on the orders will be much more important to the distributors than improving their inventory turns. No wonder the managers could not predict the positive reaction of their distributors. Still, in this case, the management experience did encompass the inventory-turns measurement, and their hesitations could be overcome by a good-enough explanation of the distributors' environment.

That is not the case when we suggested extending the replenishment solution to retail. A FMCG retailer is happy with two percent profit on sales. A FMCG retailer regards a product line that comprises five percent of his sales as a major product line. A FMCG retailer in India is used to very low gross margins (<15%). The constraint of FMCG is display space (and cash). As a result, a FMCG retailer is using, as the most important operational measurement (formally or just intuitively) the measurement of sales/shelf.

Our company's management gained their experience in a very different environment; two percent profit on sales is considered a disaster; all sales are derived from mainly two product lines; a gross margin of thirty percent is regarded as a lousy margin; the constraint is never display space (and rarely is it cash). But the biggest difference, a difference that makes extrapolation from one environment to the other almost irrelevant, is that our company's management never developed the intuition of working under the whip of the sales/shelf measurement.

No wonder that when the management of the company evaluates the likely response of retail to an offer that is based on the replenishment solution, they are bound to reach the erroneous conclusion that such an offer will be of limited attraction to retail; that any difficulty in implementing this offer will cause the retailers to reject it out of hand.

Even the best explanation of the retail environment is not sufficient to persuade the managers of the company since they lack the experience needed to check and internalize the new (to them) cause-and-effect connections. Also, an explanation is far from being enough to provide them with the solid reference base required to supply the fine details that are needed to fully adjust our suggestion to fit the specific circumstances.

When the cause-and-effect connections are based on an irrelevant extrapolation, explanations are not sufficient. If an explanation is not sufficient, what can be done to stimulate the required change?

Let's first start with what should not be done. Do not compromise. Unfortunately, when facing strong resistance—resistance that translates into "active paralysis" —the natural reaction of the people who push for the change is to compromise. This is a grave mistake. Since the tendency to compromise is so strong, and since people tend to confuse compromising with taking prudent actions to convey a message, let's elaborate on this.

A compromise would be to sweeten the offer to the retailers by augmenting the offer with some rebates or

gifts. It is a compromise because it accepts the erroneous starting point that the replenishment offer, on its
own merit, is not attractive enough to retail.

A compromise would be to use the same system used
for implementing the replenishment offer in the previous links rather than putting in the time, analysis and
efforts necessary to tailor the procedures to the specif-
ics of the retail. It is a compromise because it accepts
the erroneous starting point that the replenishment offer
will not yield big enough benefits, big enough to dwarf
the efforts needed for modifying the procedures.[*]

A compromise would be to stay with the existing frequency of delivery to retail. It is a compromise because
it accepts the erroneous starting point that the retailer
will not see the replenishment offer as attractive enough
to do some additional efforts from his side. It is a compromise because it accepts the erroneous starting point
that the replenishment offer will not yield big enough
benefits to justify increasing transportation costs. It is a
particularly bad compromise because it compromises on
the very essence of the solution; it squashes the resulting large increase in sales.

Now, I hope, what should not be done is somewhat
clearer. Never compromise on the starting point. Never
accept the erroneous cause and effect as a base for modifications or lack thereof.

---

[*]When a shop holds fewer than 20 SKUs and the quantities delivered
to one shop are a tiny fraction of a truckload, using the computerized
system that was used for distribution, rather than a prudent manual
system, is cumbersome and wasteful.

One should start with a good explanation of the new area or situation—the area or situation to which the suggested action relates and in which management does not have firsthand experience. A good explanation means giving the facts that substantiate the correct cause-and-effect connections, but not less important, proving by those facts that their current extrapolations are not valid. Don't expect full embracement of the new cause-and-effect connections. What you should expect is that management will start to doubt the validity of their extrapolated connections and start to contemplate the possibility that the connections you have presented might be plausible.

References, if they are close enough to the situation, might be helpful at this stage. Still, don't be overly surprised if they just trigger a "but our case is different" type of rejection. Even if your impression is that they have fully agreed with you, you must take into account that they do not have the needed experience and therefore it is too much to expect that they fully internalized the new cause-and-effect connections, and it is foolish to expect that they will be able to construct the required detailed modifications.

These are the reasons why the next step should be to launch a test. The test should not be regarded as a delaying tactic, which so many tests are, but as the decisive step to decide on the future actions of the company. Therefore, as part of deciding on the test the executive committee should demand to periodically review the results. Otherwise the importance of the test might deteriorate to the extent that no one will bother to even analyze the results.

It is important to design the test to accomplish two different objectives:
1. To realize the level of acceptance/rejection of the offer.
2. To get a numerical sense of the magnitude of the results, e.g. sales increase.

It is imperative to help the management in the design of such tests. Otherwise, grave mistakes are likely to happen; mistakes that might distort reality.

For example, a likely mistake on the first objective is the case where the managers of the company might not be aware that in many big stores there is a major bottleneck in the loading dock. A big store's hesitation about increasing the load at the loading dock due to excessive deliveries might be understood as hesitation on the replenishment offer, and therefore the company might get the erroneous impression that the replenishment solution is more suitable for small shops.

An example of a mistake that can occur, regarding the second objective, is not realizing in full the impact decreasing inventories has. In the large stores it is important to tie any future reduction of inventory to a commitment to preserve the current shelf space. Otherwise, the increase in sales will decay after a while. In small stores it is important to tie any future reduction of inventory to a commitment to expand on the number of different SKUs the store is holding. Otherwise, half of the potential increase in sales might not be realized.

There are many more such examples, but the real question is: When the people who are pushed outside their comfort zone don't have the experience to judge whether or not the causes and effects underlying our suggestion have merit—causes and effect that are in direct contradiction to the one they assumed—is an explanation enough to cause them to invest the considerable time and efforts needed to launch, monitor and analyze a test? Dr. W. Edwards Deming repeatedly said that it is much more difficult to rework something than to do it right the first time. In this company we reacted to the initial resistance with compromises. Reworking is needed. After losing close to one-and-a-half years, is it still possible to put things back on track?

I tried. For close to two hours I gave the explanation of the reality of retail. I explained the governing cause and effect, the role of sales/shelf. I even, at the end, gave one reference from a similar environment. I suggested a test, laid out its details, and highlighted what results should trigger which conclusions and actions.

And it worked. Within two weeks, and without any further encouragement from our side, the company had already launched a wide—much too wide—test.

I learned a lot from this case; learned in what situations it is imperative to insist on tests. To my delight, I didn't have to change my opinion about people. People's behavior is not arbitrary. Open-minded people will not necessarily agree with me, not when my arguments don't make sense to them. But open-minded people do listen, and if I explain (and when it is important) they are willing to invest in reevaluating their cause-and-effect connections.

CHAPTER 18

Emotion, Intuition and Logic

"Father, I do understand that whatever we talked about is just the beginning. I'm aware that there are specific techniques to think faster and more clearly; techniques that are tailored to specific situations. Some of them I've been using for years, many more I just heard about. I am also aware that what we have discussed has ramifications on many topics that we haven't touched. But there is still one thing that bothers me. Bothers me to the extent that I suspect there is a fundamental flaw in the approach you are exposing to me."

"Excellent," he says. "I didn't waste our time. At a minimum you've learned not to accept anything just because someone, anyone, says it with authority. Always be on guard, always think, and continuously check if reality confirms your assumptions and conclusions."

"That is exactly what bothers me. As a psychologist I'm trained to focus on people's emotions and inhibitions, but for you everything is just cold, factual logic."

"Mmm... If that is your impression maybe there was a fundamental flaw; a flaw in my explanation."

He immerses himself in the ceremony of cleaning and refilling his pipe. I just wait patiently. Finally he starts. "Efrat, logic doesn't exist in a vacuum. To perform any logical step we need to jump-start and constantly feed the logic with connections that are raised by our intuition. Haven't you noticed that the only way we can come up with a hypothesis or with a predicted effect is by intuition? And how do you expose an assumption? Again by intuition."

I still haven't gotten an answer so I wait for him to continue.

"And intuition stems from emotion. For things we don't care about, we have zero intuition. In short, we as human beings are standing on a three-legged stool: emotion, intuition and logic. To really see how everything that we've talked about ties together let's start with emotion. Every human being has emotions."

"Yes," I agree, "but that doesn't mean that we're all the same. Different people have their emotions geared toward different things. People have different areas of interest. That's why the opportunities and achievements that are important to one person may be very different from the ones that are important to another."

"Exactly. And that observation highlights something very important. You, like every other person, have your strongest intuition in the areas that are the most important to you. Isn't it comforting?"

"Yes, it is. But Father, that doesn't yet mean that I have enough intuition to achieve what I want."

"So you just have to develop it," he answers.

Before I have the chance to drag him into the debate of the extent to which intuition and brainpower can be developed, he asks me a question. "Have you noticed that when you used logic in an area, and as a result you gained a deeper understanding in that area, or even better, as a result you succeeded in removing a root conflict and substantially improving the situation, something else was also happening? Your emotions in that area intensified."

"Of course I've noticed it. More than once." I eagerly wait for him to continue.

"Look at the unavoidable result of constantly practicing thinking clearly. Naturally, when we practice thinking clearly we don't devote the same attention to every subject; we tend to concentrate on our areas of interest. Now suppose that we use the intuition that we have in these areas to fuel logic. The more we succeed in thinking clearly the deeper our emotions in those areas become. The deeper the emotions, the stronger is the resulting intuition. The stronger the intuition, the higher the chances to successfully apply logic; the higher the chances to achieve good results. And since these results were achieved in our areas of interest, they are meaningful in our eyes. The more meaningful the results, the deeper are the emotions, and so on and on."

I think about that. "What you describe is a helix that swirls upwards. Now I see why you are so convinced that everybody has enough brainpower and intuition to reach a full life. No matter what the starting levels of brainpower and intuition, if we practice thinking clearly, the helix will intensify them to new heights. Father, your approach to life is the most optimistic I have ever heard."

"Optimistic? I'm one of the most paranoid people I know. I never leave things to chance. I always try to make sure that the deck is stacked in my favor. I put safety nets on top of safety nets. Me optimistic? How did you come to such a conclusion?"

I smile and start to count on my fingers, "One, people are good. Two, every conflict can be removed. Three, every situation, no matter how complex it initially looks, is exceedingly simple. Four, every situation can be substantially improved; even the sky is not the limit. Five, every person can reach a full life. Six, there is always a win-win solution. Shall I continue to count?"

He smiles. "Efrat, do you know what an optimist with experience is?"

"A pessimist?"

"That is one possible answer. The other is 'a practical visionary.' What you will become is your choice. And Efrat, as optimistic as it all may sound, don't confuse it with being easy. You see, the other side of all the points you counted is that you can no longer find refuge in blaming others, or blaming circumstances, or saying that it's out of your control or even outside your abilities. You have to take full responsibility for your life. This will lead you to a full life but certainly not to an easy life. As a matter of fact I had to give up on the greatest pleasure of human beings, on the pleasure gained from bitching and moaning."

Laughing, I assure him, "That's a price I'm willing to pay."

Appendix

Freedom of Choice[*]
A report from Eli Goldratt to the Goldratt Group

I'm used to a relatively fast-paced life, but the past few weeks have topped anything I've experienced before.

June 25th: It's Monday evening. I am in Holland. Thomas, the regional director of Goldratt Consulting Brazil, calls. He has a meeting on July 10th, only fifteen days away, with the president of a large chain of stores, and we don't have a document that clearly outlines our solution for retail.

Knowing that the sales pipeline in Brazil needs boosting, and hearing from Thomas that the retailer brings in over 400 million U.S. dollars in sales, I ask what his reaction would be if I wrote the retailer solution and flew to Brazil to conduct the meeting with the prospect. He responds with a resounding, YYYYEEEEESSSSS!!!!

---

[*] A report to the Goldratt Group, July 2007. I use such reports to foster our culture of critically evaluating how to do better. So, even though the report is accurate in every fact, its style is not what one expects from a corporate document. For the purpose of this book it was slightly modified to enable easy comprehension for readers who are not familiar with the operations of the Goldratt Group.

I continue, "To write, urgently, such a big document and to fly halfway around the world for just one two-hour meeting doesn't make too much sense. Can you arrange for three more meetings with other retailers?"

Thomas' short answer is, "I'm already working on it."

I ask for forty-eight hours to decide. Less than an hour later, Javier, the regional director of Goldratt Consulting Latin America, is on the phone. He has a meeting with a 50-million-dollar retailer in Colombia on July 9th. What a coincidence. For four years we haven't had one single meeting with a retailer, and now we have two, back-to-back. I tell him about my conversation with Thomas and start to contemplate the possibility of reaching Brazil through Colombia.

June 27th: On Wednesday afternoon, Lisa, my technical assistant, joins us in Nottingham. Tomorrow I'll be giving the last day of an MBA program entitled "TOC for Health." But today we still have a few hours before I have to give an evening presentation to a gathering of 150 people. There is no smoking in the hotel so we (my son, Rami, Lisa and I) are sitting in a pub. In the future, I'll have to find another solution since four days from now the non-smoking epidemic will be enforced in all public places in England, including pubs. "Should I go to Brazil?" I ask.

We have a seminar scheduled in Brazil on August 17th and due to some glitches I'm concerned it will be a waste of my time; the current organizer is far from being sure that he can meet our minimum requirements—bringing in high-level people from 30 companies. But if I am able to induce the president of the store chain to recommend the seminar to its suppliers, my trip to Brazil in July will ensure a well-attended seminar in August. One hour later, once it is confirmed it will be possible to rearrange my schedule, the decision is made.

June 30th: Thomas has already arranged meetings with five retailers. The largest retailer is an 8-billion-dollar company and the smallest just 2 billion dollars. Even though we have a lot of experience in supply-chains, including retailers, until now we have never presented our solution to large retailers. I ask him to stop arranging more meetings "Let's not experiment on a grander scale."

Thomas had definitely delivered, now I had better do my part. I'm writing under Lisa's whip.

July 6th: With still a few hours to spare, the retailer "tree," the document that details the logical structure of the retailer solution, is ready. I am proud of the end result. Rather than going to Colombia, I spend two hours on Skype™ with Javier explaining how to present the retailer tree. I make him swear to report back to me, in as much detail as he remembers, about the meeting with his relatively small retailer. I want to be fully prepared before having meetings with five of the largest retailers in Brazil.

July 8th: The roller coaster starts as soon as we land in Sao Paulo. Thomas updates me on how they arranged for the meetings. The bottom line is that soon after we talked he found out that the retailer he originally had a meeting with on July 10th couldn't make it. So they actually started with zero meetings scheduled. They have never worked with retailers and didn't have any connections. Experience shows that, without prior connections, it usually takes months to arrange a two-hour meeting with a top manager of a large organization.

Having nothing to lose, Thomas and his team composed the dream list of the top ten retailers in Sao Paulo and decided to focus only on them. They were searching for friends who had friends who knew somebody, anybody (no matter how low-level), in any one of the retailers. Through these "connections" they succeeded in talking with low-level people from the retailers. They explained the purpose of the meeting: Dr. Goldratt would like to check his solution for retailers with people who have broad experience and knowledge in retail. Once they got a hesitant, or less than hesitant, response that the contact person would check the possibility of a meeting with his boss, they followed up with a letter.

It escalated to the extent that in five days they had five meetings (and three more pending on me giving more meeting dates) out of the original list of ten. The meetings were scheduled with top management—either the president or VPs of purchasing and/or merchandising. In retail these two VPs hold most of the power; one decides which products to purchase and the other decides what space and price will be allocated to each product.

It was astonishing. If meetings with such high-level people, for such big companies, can be arranged with such speed and without any real prior connections, then we are drastically underestimating our reputation. What can stop us from emulating it everywhere else? Nothing in their actions was specific to Brazil; the retailers in Brazil are no different than retailers in other regions in the world; our Theory of Constraints (TOC) is not better known in Brazil; our people in other regions are just as knowledgeable and driven....

I force myself to stop thinking about the big picture and concentrate on the task at hand. We are going to meet with very large companies. How am I going to over-come their tendency—almost conditioning—to proceed through a series of validation tests, or "pilots"?

If they start to contemplate pilots we don't stand a chance of convincing them to immediately refer their suppliers to next month's seminar.

What can help is the fact that the logic of our solution (once explained) is obvious. And it is supported by so many facts; facts that any retailer is intimately familiar with. Maybe they will realize that pilots are going to just verify the obvious; that pilots will not add anything of substance but will certainly delay getting the bottom-line results. Moreover, any retailer already considers its suppliers' performance as not good enough; they are already inclined to take actions to encourage their suppliers to improve.

Will it be enough to overcome their pilot mentality? I doubt it. What am I missing?

I don't sleep well that night. It must just be the jet lag.

July 9th: I slowly go over the solution with our local team. There is so much material in it that is new to them and I want them to radiate confidence to the prospects. Our people are used to looking at the supply chain from a supplier's perspective, so they have some difficulty view-ing the same supply chain from the other end—from the shops' perspectives. But once they adjust to it we are able to examine the main differences between this solution and our other solutions. Straightening operations in retail is simple relative to production (and a real piece of cake relative to projects), and there is no need to do any sales and marketing activities; in retail, the improved operation automatically translates into increased sales.

The ease of getting results and the magnitude of the results are astonishing. I'm wondering why I never explicitly explained it. Actually, I never highlighted it even to myself. Well, Einstein was right: "Two things are infinite: the universe and human stupidity; and I'm not sure about the universe."

We are going over the financial implications. Our fees are connected to actual results achieved and are set to be equal to about ten percent of the increase in the value of the company; no wonder our contracts are for many millions. Still, I feel uneasy when I apply our standard formulas to the huge retailers that we will be meeting. In retail it is so easy to more than double our client's percent profit on sales, therefore our fees come out to be unreasonably high. We redo the numbers trying to be as conservative as we can without being plain stupid. Then we cut it by half. It doesn't help. I decide to stop playing with the numbers.

One thing is clear: The next two days' meetings are important, more important than I originally realized. I am determined to be as prepared as I can be. It is quite uncomfortable to operate with such high uncertainty when the stakes are so high. What have I missed? What else can I do to secure the desired outcome?

It's eight o'clock in the evening and, at last, we get a call from Javier. His tone of voice is enough to indicate that his meeting went extremely well, but the line is lousy to the extent that I give up on immediate interrogation and instead ask for a written report. We'll have to wait until the morning for the details.

July 10th: What should I do first, brush my teeth or read Javier's report?

It's far better than I'd hoped for. Javier's meeting validated all the speculations that I made when I wrote the tree (the logical layout of the solution), struggling to see the world through a retailer's eyes. No, I was not sure about it; only a fool expects a prototype to work perfectly the first time.

From Javier's report it is clear that the prospect did not raise any objections; all remarks were either supporting the claims of the tree or raising a concern that was decisively answered in the next pages. Javier had conducted the meeting masterfully. No wonder that he ends his e-mail to me with: "I expect no less from you." That's a tall order.

At ten o'clock the first meeting starts. It's with the purchasing director (VP) and his three main lieutenants of a 2-billion-dollar subsidiary of an international retailer. I have to be careful since it is so easy to give purchasing managers the impression that the solution condemns them personally; that they are the Directly Responsible People for the current problems. The first step is to set the stage correctly—to bridge the gap between the grand picture I want to unfold through the tree and whatever expectations they had formed by the way the meeting was organized. "Dr. Goldratt would like to check his solution for retailers with people who have broad experience and knowledge in retail."

I've meticulously prepared myself, so what's left is to find out if what I've planned will actually work. I start by stating that what will be covered in this meeting is their choice.

"Shall I restrict myself to just the purchasing function? Should I expand it to cover the full supply chain, or..." I look directly into the eyes of the VP, owing to the fact that he is a member of the board of directors of this reputable company, "...should I expose the real thing—my suggested strategy and tactics for their company?" My words, tone of voice and body language don't leave him much choice. He prudently chooses the third alternative. From there on I'm sailing in charted waters, replicating the approach that Javier took. To my relief, the response of the four of them basically echoes the positive responses that Javier described.

I finish the meeting stating my two expectations: that they will arrange a meeting for Thomas with their president, and that they will approach their suppliers and recommend that they come to my seminar. Since this retail chain is selling its own brand of fashion clothes, their suppliers are mainly contractors—four hundred of them. They do not commit but make all the positive noises. I have conducted many such meetings and this is certainly a very good one.

We got a second, decisive verification that the solution is appealing to retailers, but I'm still not sure if I've made the right choice. I've elected not to raise, at all, the subject of gaining confidence through pilots. Should I address this more explicitly? I'm not too concerned; the meeting went so well that, in the worst case, Thomas can smoothly proceed, by following our well-established process, to move large companies. The real question is: are they going to move on their suppliers? The seminar is just one month away, so we don't have to wait long before we'll know the answer. I love the business world; it is a dream world for a scientist. In physics one has to wait (and work hard) for years before a predicted effect can be checked, and here it is just a matter of weeks.

We are waiting for the next meeting to start when it turns out that due to a scheduling mix-up it will be postponed until tomorrow. It's fine with me. Later, the extent to which Murphy can use secretaries to confuse timetables will be fully unfolded.

Sitting in the lobby, Thomas checks his text messages and, in the middle of a pretty good joke, interrupts us. He has two messages from suppliers of this morning's retailer. So they did move. And so quickly! It has been only six hours since they left. We sit quietly trying to digest the ramifications....

We still have four meetings with larger retailers ahead of us. It is conceivable that we will have three hundred companies in the seminar. Thomas calls the seminar organizer. "Not to worry," he tells us, "we'll have enough seats even if the organizer has to build the hall himself."

How many more Goldratt Consulting (GC) auditors do we need? The auditors are our most knowledgeable people and it takes over a year to bring even an experienced person to that level. Currently we have two auditors in Brazil and, until ten minutes ago, I was convinced that the auditors' capacity would not be a problem until the end of 2008.

But what if what we see is real? I'm starting to realize the extent to which we are not ready for success and how quickly it can hit us.

July 11th: We gather in the conference room. Thomas informs us that he got a call from yesterday's prospect. They went over our seminar brochure and noticed that in two days the early-bird price will no longer be available. They asked for an extension and for a special code for their suppliers to register. They wouldn't have asked for this unless they intend to approach all their suppliers. Now three hundred suppliers in the seminar doesn't sound so farfetched.

I contemplate the ramifications. Usually, half the companies that attend a seminar apply for a project. The fact that *these* attendees are coming because of a strong recommendation from their important client will only help to increase the number of applicants. In the past we did not move most applicants to the next step because so many of the companies were not a good enough fit with our standard solutions. But in this case the fit is almost guaranteed; we know a priori that they do fit the consumer-goods solution. That means that this seminar can yield over 150 prospects. Who is going to conduct the meetings? And what about…? And if so…?

"Something is wrong," I conclude, and call Rami. I give him the bare facts and ask him to come back to me with just one number. Conservatively, how many GC auditors will we need for Brazil within a year from today?

The next meeting is with a department store chain with sales of over $8 billion a year. When the director (VP) of merchandising tells us that shortages (out-of-stocks) are over twenty-five percent, I know that we are going to go through a pleasant repeat. And we do. He responds extremely well to my suggestion to send their suppliers to the seminar. They have fourteen thousand, yes, *fourteen thousand* suppliers.

We receive Rami's answer: ten auditors. "Tell him about the meeting that just ended," I suggest. Five minutes later, Rami's response is, "Add a zero." That sentence continues to echo in my head.

The next meeting doesn't start on time. Murphy strikes again and again. Stupid things like secretaries giving the wrong meeting place or the wrong date and, due to terrible traffic in Sao Paulo and these people's heavy schedules, it is practically impossible to rectify. The end result is that we finish with just three meetings out of five. Thomas and his team are embarrassed and irritated but I don't let it cloud their grand achievement.

Late afternoon we have what turns out to be our last meeting. It's a larger, direct competitor of the first prospect, with four billion dollars in annual sales. The meeting goes as smoothly as the previous ones. They agree to arrange a meeting with their president. The director of purchasing states that he will contact their suppliers—four thousand of them—and makes sure that he has all the seminar material.

On my flight home to Israel I decide to do my best to

ensure that all the top managers of the Goldratt Group join together. No matter what they had scheduled for the 19th and 20th of July they must come to my office in Holland.

WE—who warn all our clients that capitalizing on a competitive edge leads, unavoidably, to an increase in sales that, if unprepared for, can easily destroy the competitive edge and the company.

WE— haven't done what we preach!!!

I'm deeply disappointed with myself.

July 19th: Everybody is in Holland. In five minutes we will start. I quickly check my e-mails. The e-mail from Thomas hits me right between the eyes.

He has succeeded in contacting only two out of the three retailers we met. And both informed him that they are not yet ready to arrange a meeting with their president. And, until they know more about the content of my seminar, they are not going to approach their suppliers in any major way. In retrospect that is what one expects from a director of a large company; the careful, risk-avoidance, pilot mentality.

But now, three minutes before the gathering of all the top people of the Goldratt Group, I don't have time or patience for retrospection.

At this point there are usually two alternatives:

One choice is to behave like a kid whose prized toy was brutally taken away or like an adult who comes to claim his big prize in the lottery just to find out that one number is different. In short, "Life's a bitch and then you die."

The other choice is to examine where we stand. To realize that in the last three weeks:

1.Reality just vividly demonstrated what should be our most perfect target market—retail.

2.Reality just pointed us in the direction of the most powerful multiplier—one retailer leads to numerous suppliers.

In short, reality just showed us a very effective way to capitalize on our already built competitive edge.

3.Reality just spared us from floundering under an avalanche.

4.All the ingredients are lined up for us to get everything we wanted and then some, in a planned and controlled way.

In short, reality just highlighted to us how important it is to plan our actions to ensure that we sustain the exponential growth.

Two alternatives: one is to bitch about reality and the other is to harvest the gifts it just gave us. This is what I call the *freedom of choice*.

We spend the next two days constructing the (now obvious) process to capitalize and sustain. But that is the subject of another report.